NEVER SETTLE FOR LESS

10 Trucking Case Truths You Need to Know
(That Your Insurance Company Will Never Tell You)

DINO COLOMBO

WEST VIRGINIA'S PREMIER TRUCK ACCIDENT ATTORNEY

Never Settle for Less

10 Trucking Case Truths
You Need to Know
(That Your Insurance Company Will Never Tell You)

Dino S. Colombo

Never Settle for Less:
10 Trucking Case Truths You Need to Know
(That Your Insurance Company Will Never Tell You)

Dino S. Colombo
Colombo Law
341 Chaplin Road, 2nd Floor
Morgantown, WV 26501
(304) 599-4229
Toll Free: (888) 860-1414
http://www.callcolombolaw.com

Front cover image © Lucian Bobotan
(http://www.123rf.com/profile_lucianbobotan)

ISBN-10: 1-946203-10-6
ISBN-13: 978-1-946203-10-6

—Disclaimer—
Although the author and publisher have made
every effort to ensure that the information in
this book was correct at press time, the author
and publisher do not assume and hereby
disclaim any liability to any party for any loss,
damage, or disruption caused by errors or
omissions, whether such errors or omissions
result from negligence, accident, or any other
cause.

**Expert
Press**
www.ExpertPress.net

Table of Contents

Introduction

A Hidden Epidemic

What would you say if I told you that trucking collisions are an unrecognized epidemic in our country? I suspect that you would find that hard to believe. Prove it, you might tell me. That's what I want to do in this book: to show you how widespread this epidemic is, and to give you the vital information that will help protect you and your family if you become involved in such a collision.

I want to begin by telling you a story.

It was an ordinary spring evening, about 7:30 p.m. Donna Collins of Clarksburg, West Virginia was on her way to visit her grandfather. Her route took her along Old Bridgeport Hill Road. When she reached the intersection of Old Bridgeport Hill and US Route 50, she stopped for the red traffic light. When her light turned green, Donna proceeded into the intersection to make a left-hand turn onto US Route 50 East.

At the same time, headed west in the westbound lane of US Route 50, there was a Dodge Ram 4500 heavy duty pickup truck pulling a 20-foot steel trailer. Moving at 50 mph, the truck hit Donna Collins squarely on her driver's side door, knocking her car about 60 feet.

The date was April 1, 2015. And on that ordinary spring evening, Donna Collins' life was changed forever. She was 46 years old.

Donna was trapped in the car for about 45 minutes. She was unresponsive and had to be extricated from her vehicle. She was taken by ambulance to United Hospital Center in Bridgeport, West Virginia, where emergency room staff recognized that she was in respiratory failure and intubated her. She had a fractured back, a fractured femur, and numerous other injuries. The Health Net helicopter service life-flighted her to the trauma center at West Virginia University Hospital.

Donna Collins' car

Due to the respiratory failure and the severity of her other injuries, Donna was unconscious and in a coma-type state for several weeks. She was eventually transferred to a specialty hospital that cared for patients who were dependent on a ventilator. After a time she was able to be weaned off the ventilator. She was moved to a rehab hospital, and then to a nursing home. Donna's family was not satisfied with the nursing home care, so they finally decided to bring her home.

Donna Collins suffered a severe traumatic brain injury that prevents her from taking care of herself. She needs attendant care; someone needs to be with her 24 hours a day, seven days a week. Because of her brain injury, she now has a very poor memory. We call it "five minute brain." You tell her something, and five minutes later, you have to repeat it. She does not have any insight into her condition. She thinks that she can walk when she cannot. She's basically confined to a wheelchair or a walker.

She was severely injured. Along with the traumatic brain injury, she suffered a fractured femur and a T4 chance fracture that required a cervical fusion. She also had a number of other orthopedic-related injuries: broken ribs, torn labrum in her shoulder, and a knee injury.

The Collins family contacted us, and we got involved immediately. The key to these things is getting on the case early, and fortunately, the family called us the day after the accident. That same day, we had an accident reconstructionist on the way to West Virginia to begin the gathering of evidence and the reconstructing of the accident.

That's especially important when you're dealing with a commercial motor vehicle. In this case, that Dodge Ram 4500 is considered a commercial motor vehicle. That means that it is governed by the Federal Motor Carrier Safety Regulations.

Most people think of a commercial motor vehicle as the 18-wheeler they see on the interstate. While that certainly is a commercial motor vehicle, there are many other commercial motor vehicles that you might not recognize as such. A Ford F250 can be a commercial motor vehicle. The garbage truck, the tow truck, the bus, the van that transports people to and from the airport—those are all commercial motor vehicles, and they're governed by the Federal Motor Carrier Safety Administration. People who are injured or who are the victims of an accident or a collision involving one of these large trucks need a law firm that knows the difference between a commercial motor vehicle and a personal vehicle. There are extensive rules and regulations that govern a commercial motor vehicle—CMV for short—and they are completely different than those for a personal vehicle.

The Federal Motor Carrier Safety Administration puts out an extensive handbook that details these rules and regulations. There are many regulations involving the qualifications of a driver, and what a driver must do to qualify to drive these CMVs.

The driver of the truck that hit Donna Collins had been on that road hundreds of times. He later testified that he knew the light was there, he knew the intersection was there, and as he approached the intersection, he was doing approximately 50 mph. He said the sun was in his eyes and he couldn't see the color of the light, so he entered the intersection having no idea whether the light was red, yellow, or green. Instead of stopping, or slowing down, or pulling over, he just blew right through the intersection, and hit Donna Collins at 50 mph.

At first, the Collins case sounded like just a guy who had run a stoplight. It happens every day. But as we dug into the case, it turned out to be so much more than a simple stoplight case.

In my settlement video that I sent to the insurance company, I made it very clear that this case was about warning signs and stoplights, but not just that warning sign and stoplight on US Route 50 and Old Bridgeport Hill Road. It was the warnings and stoplights that the company had blown through for the months and the years leading up to April 1, 2015. The company that owned the truck was an out-of-state natural gas service company that provided containment services to the companies that drill the wells. This company had come to West Virginia from Pennsylvania to profit off of the fracking boom that is going on in West Virginia and Ohio.

In the natural gas industry, and specifically throughout West Virginia and Ohio, there's much more to natural gas well sites than just the drilling. The well sites involve many different kinds of companies and many different people. It's not just the drilling company. The particular company that was at fault in this case wasn't the company that actually drilled the hole. They were what's called a containment company; they provided environmental services to the fracking company. If there's a spill of water, of sand, of chemicals, or whatever at the site, the containment company provides services to try to make sure that that spill doesn't contaminate the water or the property.

This particular containment company was a startup company that rushed into West Virginia to try to make a quick dollar on the natural gas boom. They were in a hurry to get started and get a crew together, so they could get out there and start making money. Now let's be clear, making money is not a bad thing. But when any company puts profit over safety, disastrous results are almost certain to occur.

The stoplights that this company blew through prior to April 1, 2015 involved the hiring of this particular driver. Because they were in a hurry to get to work in the gas fields, and they were a startup company, they had basically stolen a crew from another company. They knew these guys from other associations, and brought a number of them in from another company. They never even interviewed the driver who later hit Donna Collins, let alone did the required background check. All they knew was that he had been working for another company as a driver.

The company didn't have an employment application; they didn't do an interview. They didn't check his employment history. They didn't check his driving history. They didn't check his criminal background. They didn't check anything. They needed a driver, and he was a driver for another company. The thought process was this: We've got to have a driver and we've got to have a driver yesterday—not today, but yesterday—so we'll take you. And so he drove. He was the driver of a commercial motor vehicle.

Why do all these things matter? The Federal Motor Carrier Safety Administration has specific rules that a motor carrier—the owner of a trucking company—must follow before they put a driver behind the wheel of one of their commercial motor vehicles. The motor carrier is supposed to have the applicant's name, address, date of birth, social security number. They had none of that. The company is supposed to have the addresses at which the applicant resided during the three years preceding the date of his employment application. For this guy they didn't even have an employment application.

That's just the start. The motor carrier is supposed to have the applicant's employment history, to know where this person has worked for the past number of years. The carrier is supposed to have the issuing state number and expiration of each unexpired commercial motor vehicle operator's license the applicant holds. This company didn't have any of that. They're supposed to have a list of all motor vehicle accidents in which the applicant was involved during the three years preceding his employment, and a list of all violations of motor carrier or motor vehicle laws. They had none of that.

The carrier is supposed to look at the applicant's driving history: Has the applicant ever had his license revoked?

The carrier is supposed to get a criminal background check: Has the applicant ever had any criminal convictions?

The motor carrier in the Collins case had done none of these things.

The key to this particular case centered on the issue of a license revocation for this particular driver many years earlier and the facts and circumstances surrounding that revocation. Why was this so important? Several years prior to this accident, this driver had been convicted of not just one, but *two* DUIs. In fact, on the day he was hired for this job, he was a fugitive from justice because he had not completed the required alcohol awareness education programs and had not paid his fines from his previous DUI convictions. He was a fugitive from justice and he knew that he was.

He admitted to all of this in his deposition—that he had two previous DUIs and that he was a fugitive from justice. This is how he realized that he was considered a fugitive. He went to a Dick's Sporting Goods store to buy himself a deer rifle. Dick's Sporting Goods is a big outdoor retailer here in West Virginia and Ohio which also sells guns, hunting rifles, shotguns, ammo, and that kind of thing. When Dick's did the background check on him for his rifle purchase, the background check showed that there was a warrant out for his arrest. He was detained at Dick's.

So the people at Dick's knew about his record. We did a 20 minute Google search on this guy and found out about his DUIs, criminal history and that he was a fugitive from justice but his employer didn't know about any of it. When I hit him with all of this stuff in his deposition, he willingly admitted to all of it. Yes, he was convicted twice of DUI; yes, he was a fugitive from justice with a warrant out for his arrest; no, the company had never asked him about his driving history. No, the company had never asked him about his criminal history, and he did have one, that included destruction of property when he was a younger man in his late teens and early 20s. So he had a criminal history, he had the two DUIs, he was a fugitive with an outstanding warrant, and he very freely admitted to all of that. He testified that no one at the company had ever asked him. He didn't try to hide any of his history from anybody but no one ever interviewed him. He didn't fill out an application. He just went to work.

I know it sounds ridiculous. I was speechless. The driver was very upfront about it. He said, "Yes, I did have two DUIs. Yes, I didn't finish the education that I was supposed to. I didn't pay the fines. There's a warrant out for my arrest." And I said, "That was your status the day you were hired with this company, you had all of that going on?" His answer was, "Yes." I said, "If anyone at the company had asked you, what would you have told them?" He said, "I would have told them the truth. I didn't have anything to hide." He says that now, but whether he would have, who knows?

Our position, of course, was that he never should have been behind the wheel of a commercial motor vehicle on April 1,

2015. He never should have been hired to drive a commercial motor vehicle to begin with. If they wanted to hire him as a laborer, fine. But don't put him behind the wheel of a Dodge 4500 Ram heavy duty pickup truck pulling a 20-foot steel trailer and designate him as the driver of your CMV. This is a safety-sensitive position that requires the driver to be responsible and conscientious. It requires someone who realizes the important role he or she has. Not someone who has been convicted of two DUIS and is a fugitive from justice.

The company was negligent first in hiring this guy as a driver, but also, and perhaps more importantly, in putting him back on the road after an accident. You see after they hired him, and before the accident with Donna Collins, he was in another accident. He rear-ended somebody, and he also got a speeding ticket. Both of those things occurred in one of the company's trucks. Because of the speeding ticket and the collision, the company required him to take a defensive driving course. He was reprimanded, and according to the rules and regulations under his reprimand he was to complete a defensive driving course within 20 days. Had he followed the rules of his reprimand he would have completed the course about 30 days *before* his collision with Donna Collins.

He started the course, and he claims—and testified under oath in his deposition—that as he was actually sitting at the computer taking the online defensive driving course and the company told him to stop. They stopped him in the middle of the course, and told him that he needed to go out on a job. He stopped in the middle of taking this defensive driving course and never finished it. The company knew that he hadn't finished it, and they put him back out on the road. He still hadn't finished the course as of the date of the Collins accident, which occurred about 30 days later. Even as of the date of the deposition, which was approximately nine months after the accident, he had not completed the defensive driving course. I asked him about it. I said, "Did the company know that you had not completed the course that they required you to take?" He said, "Absolutely. Not only did they know it, they're the reason I didn't complete it."

The company had an expert witness who was supposed to testify that their conduct had been appropriate. Believe it or not, I got their own expert witness, who they never should have had, to testify that their conduct had been inappropriate. Under oath for the defendant, this witness testified that the company was not only negligent, but they were also reckless. They put profit over safety by pulling this guy out of the class and putting him back on the road. The Federal Motor Carrier Safety Administration and the rules and regulations that govern motor carriers were the linchpin of that case.

It was crazy. The company lied about so many things. They are supposed to keep what's called a driver qualification file. It's just evidence that you actually did what you're supposed to do, that you've complied with all the rules and regulations. This company claimed that they had a driver qualification file on this guy, but for reasons they couldn't explain, they couldn't find it. They wanted to testify what was in it, even though it wasn't available for anyone to see. The judge said no. The company knew they were in trouble. We knew they were in trouble, but they were trying anything and everything to avoid admitting their misconduct. Believe it or not, the company even tried to blame Donna Collins. They admitted that the truck driver's light was red, and they admitted that Donna's light was green, but they said that it was really her fault. They said she should have recognized as she entered that intersection that the truck driver was not going to stop and she should have stopped her car before he hit her.

I said, "Thank you. Thank you for making such a ridiculous and offensive allegation. Thank you."

The incident itself was clear liability. The guy blew through a traffic light. There were multiple witnesses. The company was dead in the water as far as their own conduct went, just because they were in a hurry.

You hear these stories all the time about people putting profit over safety, and you think that these are just allegations. There is no way this could be true. It is true and it happens far more than you might think. The Donna Collins case is a classic example of "profit over safety". Donna Collins' case resulted in a settlement of $18,250,000 and even though this is a great deal of money her life will never be the same.

That was a large settlement, but these accidents are not unusual. All you need to do is look at the newspaper, or turn on your local TV news. You see one truck accident after another, after another. They involve gas well trucks, tractor trailers, water trucks, garbage trucks, all these commercial motor vehicles. Why? Money. Money is the incentive for all of it.

Look at the Donna Collins case. Capstone Energy Services needed a driver. They didn't even care who the driver was. They didn't care about his background. They just needed somebody to drive. Because if they don't have a designated driver, in those circumstances, that truck can't go anywhere and they can't make their money.

If the driver has to pull over because there is a problem with the vehicle and it has to be serviced, they are losing money. If drivers have to spend the night somewhere because they have already timed out, because they've driven too much and worked too long, the company is losing money. The financial incentive for these companies is always to skirt the rules, or break the rules, or try to get around the rules, and hope that nothing unfortunate happens.

When something does happen—and it inevitably does—it's people like Donna Collins who pay the terrible price for these companies' incentives. Donna was just going about her regular day. There was nothing unusual or untoward about it. She wasn't drinking. She wasn't going out with her friends. She was heading to see her grandfather. She was just going about her day, living her life.

I can't restore that life she was living. I work on the principle that you can never rewind, but you can reassemble. I can't go back in time and tell Donna Collins not to drive into that intersection because that guy is going to blow right through it. But because her family contacted us immediately, what I could do, and what we were able to do, was to get a life-care plan put together for her, and force the insurance company to pay for that life-care plan. She is taken care of the rest of her life. She will get the physical therapy that she needs. She will get the attendant care that she will need for the rest of her life. She will get a handicapped-accessible home so that she doesn't have to struggle to get in and out of the bath tub, or to go to the bathroom, or do her daily activities. She will be able to have a bed that is comfortable for her.

We can't rewind the clock and bring back a loved one who has been lost, or make the injury go away, but we can help the victims and survivors have a more comfortable and enjoyable life.

That's the purpose of this book, to help people understand the real truth about trucking cases so that they can be prepared in the event of a truck collision. It's for the person who has been involved, or whose family member or friend has been involved, in a collision with some kind of large truck. It might be a tractor trailer; it might be the natural gas service truck. It could be the garbage truck or the commercial van or the box truck or delivery truck.

One of the most basic things that people need to understand is that the trucking company, and the insurance companies for the trucking company, and the lawyers for the trucking company are never there to protect the interest of the injured person, or the family of the deceased person. They are there to protect the interests of the trucking company and their own interest, and they are there to settle the case as quickly and as cheaply as they can.

It doesn't mean that they will be openly adversarial. They're going to be nice to all of these victims. They're going to seem nice and caring to the wife of a man who lost his life. They're going to seem very sympathetic, and they're going to be nice to Donna Collins, with her severe brain injury, but the reality is they want to settle this case, or any case, for a fraction of what it is worth. I want people to understand how much there is to these cases. They can be so complicated and such a fight. You have to be prepared to go the distance. Do not expect the insurance company for the trucking company to take care of you. You need to hire a lawyer who represents you and your family and who will be there to protect you and your interests.

The Donna Collins case is a prime example. At first it looked like a run-of-the-mill case: A guy who wasn't paying attention and ran through a stop light. That run-of-the-mill case would have been worth a fraction of what it eventually turned out to be. What changed was that we were able to discover the real history behind the case and the underlying causes that contributed to the collision. It wasn't just a driver who happened to be not paying attention that day. It was a driver with a history of not paying attention. It was a company with a history of not paying attention. It was a company with a history of putting profit over safety. All of those factors made that case much more valuable and allowed us to provide the lifetime care that Donna Collins needs.

These are complicated cases. Commercial motor vehicles and their drivers are subject to a maze of rules and regulations. The average person may be able to read and understand the rules, but they lack the experience to know what rules and regulations apply in a given case. These aren't some mystic rules that only some sophisticated lawyer is capable of reading, but the average person would have no reason to know these rules even exist, let alone which of these hundreds and hundreds of rules apply. That's our job. That's what people pay us to do. That's our expertise: to learn the rules, to understand which rules apply, and to determine which rules may have been broken.

These trucking cases are not accidents at all. I think that word is used way too loosely. These are not accidents. The Donna Collins case was not an accident. It was a collision. It was a crash. It was a tragedy. It wasn't an accident. It could have been avoided, and it should have been avoided. It was entirely preventable. Most, if not all, of these trucking cases are not accidents. They are preventable and avoidable, and no one has to die, and no one has to be disabled and no one has to experience a life time of misery. It just doesn't have to happen.

If it does happen to you, you need to know what to do. You need someone who can help you identify the rules and regulations that apply, and to discover whether those rules and regulations were violated. You may not even know whom to sue. I know it sounds crazy but identifying the proper person or company who is responsible can be very difficult. For example, who *really* owns the truck, who is responsible for maintenance and who employs the driver? These and many other questions are not always apparent.

My job as an attorney in such cases is to have the responsible parties pay their fair share and to compensate the injured person, or the decedent's family, fairly and completely. That's my job. We're not out there trying to chase people down who don't belong in our case. That's not what we're trying to do. We don't want anybody to pay an amount of money that they are not responsible for. That's not it at all.

If people don't hire the right attorney—and hire them quickly—they could be misled. They could be entrapped. They could be talked into making a deal that they will regret the rest of their lives, because once a settlement agreement is signed the case is over forever. Once you release the other party you can never come back to them and recover additional money. If you release the other party, you can't come back six months later, or a year later, or two years later, and say, "Oh, I needed this surgery that I didn't realize I was going to need, so I'm going to need some more money." That's not how this works. Once it's settled, the case is over. The decision that a person makes about who is going to represent them is crucial and can be life changing.

I want people to be able to make the right decisions. Whether they come to me or whether they go to someone else, I want my readers to be represented by someone who is competent and who has expertise in handling cases involving large trucks where someone has been severely injured or killed.

That is critically important, because the decisions that the client and their lawyer are making may well be life changing decisions. These decisions will affect and influence their lives and the lives of their children, probably the rest of their lives.

Across the United States, in 2015, there were 4,311 large trucks and buses involved in fatal crashes, an increase of eight percent over 2014. That number has increased 26 percent since 2009. (Data from the U.S. Department of Transportation, Federal Motor Carrier Services Administration Analysis Division, *Large Truck and Bus Crash Facts 2015*)

As I said at the beginning of this introduction, this is an unrecognized epidemic. All you have to do is open up the newspaper or look at the local news and you will see one truck collision after another. Every day there are people who are being severely and permanently injured, disabled, and even killed by large truck accidents. These are major catastrophes. This isn't a fender-bender that leaves you with a little bruise on your arm. In a large truck collision the injuries are seldom minor. They are usually life-changing injuries, or life-ending injuries.

I want to educate people. I want to help people make good and informed decisions about what to do if they find themselves or their loved one in a situation like this. Unfortunately, these situations are becoming more and more common.

I hope you never find yourself in a case like this. But I want you to be prepared if you do. This book is intended to provide practical advice without legal jargon. Consider it a how-to book to answer this question: What do I do if I'm involved, or a loved one is involved, in a collision with a large truck?

Chapter 1

You Need an Expert

It may seem obvious, but I think it's important to emphasize that a trucking collision is not the same as a rear-ender in front of the convenience store.

When a commercial motor vehicle is involved in a collision, the rules are different. Often the stakes are higher. In an injury case—whether it's a trucking case, or a medical malpractice case, or any other type of injury case—there are three primary criteria to be established. The first is negligence, or reckless conduct. The second is causation, meaning that the negligence caused an injury. Then the third is damages, meaning the value of that injury.

As you can see from the Donna Collins case that I described in the Introduction, there are many elements that go into establishing these three criteria. Because many are specific to trucking cases, you'll want legal representation with experience in, and a focus on, trucking cases.

The focus of our practice is in trucking cases. My team and I know what to look for in trucking cases. We know how to interpret these complicated Federal Motor Carrier Safety Regulations. We know experts in accident reconstruction. We know experts who can testify to what regulations the trucking company and the truck driver may have violated. We know experts who can evaluate the client and can prepare a reasonable and appropriate life care plans. Often times the injuries are not only physical but emotional. That is very common. We have access to experts to evaluate for traumatic brain injuries as well as emotional issues such as PTSD. We know experts who can do vocational evaluations, as well as economists who can place an appropriate value on whatever the client will need going forward.

The reason my firm knows all of these experts is that we have made this work the focus of our practice. We do not focus on family law, or on general practice, where the lawyer's day might be taken up with a will, and then a divorce, and then a DUI, and then a criminal matter, and then maybe another divorce. If their practice isn't focused on trucking cases, they are likely to find it extremely difficult to go from the divorce or the criminal case and then jump into a complicated trucking case.

For example, I don't do divorces. I don't want to do divorces. I wouldn't even know where to start in a divorce. A lot of divorce lawyers wouldn't know where to start in a trucking case. That's just not what they do.

There's a common misconception, maybe fueled a bit by TV and movies, that all lawyers and law firms handle all different kinds of cases. The reality is quite different.

There's a commercial that runs in our market, for a national firm. They give a laundry list of all of the kinds of injury claims that they will handle. There are probably 150 of them, like dog bites, bicycle accidents, swimming pools, slip and fall, medical malpractice, school-related problems, bullying—their list includes everything under the sun. At the end of it, they finally say, "We don't even care how you were hurt. Just call." They don't care. They do anything and everything.

No one can be an expert at everything. No one can know the rules and regulations of everything. Anyone who says they can is not being honest.

I see four key differences between a lawyer like me, whose practice focuses on trucking collisions, and a general practice lawyer whose practice does wills and estates and a little bit of criminal work, then picks up a divorce case and does the whole gamut of law. Those four differences are these: competency, cost, connections, and class.

Competency

A person injured or the family of someone killed by a large truck deserves a lawyer whose practice focuses on trucking cases. The defense lawyers, who handle these cases representing the trucking companies, have practices focused on defending trucking companies. They do that because those cases are so valuable, because those cases are so complicated, and because the outcome is so important. The outcome can be in the tens of millions of dollars.

So if the trucking company wants a law firm that's focused on trucking cases, doesn't the person who has been injured, or the family of someone who has been killed, deserve to have on their side a lawyer whose practice focuses on trucking cases?

In our practice, we see a handful—and only a handful—of defense firms involved in trucking cases. Those are the defense firms that focus on defending trucking companies. That's what they do. The trucking companies and their insurance carriers have them on speed dial. When the truck driver calls from his cell phone to notify the trucking company that he's been in an accident or collision with another vehicle, the trucking company and the insurance company are dispatching their lawyers at that very moment. Those guys have "chase teams" or "go teams" ready to dispatch right to the site of the accident.

I have seen defense lawyers on the site of an accident within an hour of the state trooper getting there. That's how quickly they are on these cases. That's their job. They are focused on trucking cases, they're very sophisticated, and they're very capable defense lawyers. Their job is to pay the victim or the victim's family as little as possible. That is their job, and they are very good at it.

The person who has been injured or the family of the person who has been killed needs to have a lawyer with that same focus on trucking cases. They need a lawyer who is ready to take on that insurance company, who knows the rules and regulations that govern trucks, and who has the competence, the experience, and the background to handle these cases.

Cost

Trucking cases are expensive. It is not uncommon in a trucking case for the legal expenses—the advanced out-of-pocket legal expenses—to be $100,000 to $500,000. It can be as much as a million dollars. The resources on the defense side are practically unlimited. The trucking company has a lot of money and their insurance company has a lot of money. So you need a law firm with the resources to advance those expenses and to stay the course against the defense lawyers and all of their tactics.

One of the things they will do in defending the case is to delay the case. They will see how long they can wait you out, how long can you hold on. It's hard enough for the client who has been injured to hold on. If you have a law firm that doesn't have the financial resources to advance for the case, and then to hold on as long as needed, it's no good. The law firm that advances $100,000 but needs it back in 60 days is not a law firm that you can count on to go the distance. These cases won't get resolved in 60 days. These cases will take upwards of a year, sometimes two years, sometimes longer.

If the insurance company senses that the law firm does not have the financial wherewithal, they will delay and delay because they know that if they push it out far enough, the client and the law firm will finally say "We need the money; we'll take whatever you offer." That is not our firm. We will do what it takes, for as long as it takes, to get the right result, to get the fair result, to get the result that the client deserves.

Connections

In order to establish our three criteria—negligence, causation, and damages—and reach a successful outcome, we use expert witnesses in every facet of the case. Because our firm has made trucking cases the focus of our practice for years, we have built working relationships with the best experts in this field.

The first step in any trucking case is to get the *liability experts* to evaluate the conduct of the truck driver as well as the trucking company. We need to carefully evaluate the whether the driver and/or the company was negligent or reckless. We also need to evaluate the conduct of our own client. Let's face it—not all collisions with a truck are going to be the fault of the truck driver or the company. Let's figure this out as soon as we can. Timing is crucial; the sooner the better. Physical evidence can fade away quickly, witnesses disappear, and memories get clouded. That's why I always advise people to call as soon as they can.

We start with an *accident reconstruction expert* who specializes in trucking cases. This is typically an engineer or a state trooper or retired law enforcement person who has specific training in accident reconstruction.

The reconstruction often starts with downloading the truck's computer data. Every commercial vehicle has a black box, and the data stored in it gives us an enormous amount of information concerning how fast the vehicle was going when it entered a particular intersection, how fast it was going at the time of the collision, when the brakes were applied, and much more.

What often happens in these cases, especially if the vehicle is totaled, is that the insurance company will dispose of the vehicle. It's going to be hard to reconstruct the collision without a vehicle. It's going to be hard to download the black box information from both the truck and the client's vehicle if one or both have been destroyed or thrown away or disposed of in some fashion.

That black box data is invaluable to us as we build the case, but that's just the start. We talk to the witnesses who may have seen the collision. We look at phone records for the driver of the truck. We look at text messages from the driver. We look at photographs from the accident scene. If there's a stoplight involved, we look at the sequencing of the stoplight. We measure skid marks. We look at every aspect of the accident, basically taking it from start to finish, and we reconstruct that accident so that we can, in an accurate and understandable way, explain to the client, to the court, and ultimately to a jury, why the collision occurred and what went wrong.

That's why it's so important for us to get out there quickly. You'd be surprised how fast skid marks fade away. We want to get photographs from the scene of the collision and video if it's available. We want to start interviewing witnesses immediately, while their memories are fresh and before they disappear. Since a lot of these crashes occur on large highways, many of the drivers aren't local people. They may be going on vacation, or just passing through and they live in another state. They may not want to be bothered by this, so we want to talk to them right away. We want to talk to the investigating officers immediately because if we don't get to them soon, he or she is on to the next collision, or robbery, or other incident. It's not going to be fresh in his or her mind any more. It's going to be fresh at the time. Our goal is always to get the most accurate and complete information, and that takes expertise in these reconstructions.

Along with the reconstruction expert, we also want a *trucking expert* on the case immediately. The first reconstructs what happened, while the second expert provides insight and testimony on the conduct of the motor carrier—that's a fancy name for a trucking company—and the driver.

These trucking experts specialize in what a motor carrier should do or not do or what a driver should do or not do. They know the federal motor carrier regulations forward and backward. These FMCSA rules and regulations can be complicated; the book itself is 592 pages long. What may seem to be a perfectly straightforward rule may have dozens of exceptions. We understand which exceptions apply and which exceptions do not apply. These trucking experts are the ones who help us interpret these rules. They know what is acceptable conduct by a trucking company and what is not. Likewise, the experts evaluate the conduct of the driver. After all it is the conduct of the driver that has potentially played a role in bringing about this collision.

Those rules—and there are literally hundreds of them—are what make a commercial motor vehicle collision so different from a collision with a personal vehicle. All of the rules that apply to commercial motor vehicles won't apply to a regular personal vehicle. If it had been just a personal vehicle that hit Donna Collins at the intersection of Route 50 and Old Bridgeport Hill Road, all of those rules and regulations that were violated by this trucking company wouldn't even apply. Without an expert's knowledge of the rules, the lawyer or the client may miss something that entirely changes the value of that case.

The reconstruction expert and the trucking expert not only help us address the issues of negligence but also causation. Remember we have to prove that the negligent conduct truck driver and/or the trucking company is what *caused* the collision. If the conduct of the driver or company did not cause the collision then there is no case. This can be very complicate and it is why we utilize a variety of sophisticated experts.

When we start to consider damages, there are a lot of different questions to be answered. What is the injured person going to need going forward? Are they going to recover from their injuries? If so, how long is their recovery likely to take? Are they going to need physical therapy? Will they need additional surgery? How long are they going to be out of work? Will they even be able to go back to work? Do they need to go on disability? What are we going to do about their medical expenses between the time of the collision and the time a case either gets settled or goes to trial?

To look at all of these questions, we hire *damage experts*. These damage experts come from a variety of areas. They may include life care planners, orthopedic surgeons, psychologists or psychiatrists. They can be *vocational experts* who evaluate a person to tell us whether or not they can go back to work, and if they can, what they can and cannot do. A lot of our clients work in heavy labor. After a truck collision they may be employable but often they're not going to able to go back to performing heavy labor. They may be able to go back to work in a limited duty capacity, but if they've hurt their back or their leg or their neck they can't go back and pick up a hundred pounds on a regular basis. So what can they do? You also have to consider people's age and educational background. Are they going to be re-trainable? A vocational expert helps with all of that, helping us determine what types of employment the person can and cannot do. Often they may not be able to go back to work at all. With that said, we always want our clients to do what they can to live as normal a life as possible. For example, while a client may not be able to go back to work, they may be able to volunteer at the local hospital or charity. This is helpful to the client in so many ways. It gives them a sense of worth and shows everyone that even when faced with adversity that you are willing to be productive and to help others.

When a client has suffered a catastrophic injury and can no longer live on their own or needs some form of assistance a *life care planner* is retained to help put together a long-term life-care plan. In Donna Collins' case, given her catastrophic injuries, we had a *rehabilitation expert* who helped us develop a life care plan which came to about eight million dollars. That's what it will cost to take care of her the rest of her life. We use a rehabilitation physician who has expertise as a life care planner to evaluate the client's physical condition as well as their living situation.

Donna Collins lived in a two-story home before the collision. She can't live in a two-story home now. She can't get up the stairs. The life care planner evaluates the client from not only a medical and psychological point of view but also with regard to their physical condition and living conditions. The planner then makes recommendations about what needs to be done both from a physical point of view and in terms of facilities. That may include rehabilitation care, home care, home modifications, a hospital bed, a wheelchair-accessible van, and all those kinds of things. The rehabilitation expert helps us identify all of those specific needs.

Once we have a plan, we bring in an *economist* who has to evaluate the plan's cost. Rehabilitation care, making modifications to a home or building a new home, what a vehicle is going to cost and how often that vehicle has to be maintained or replaced, the same with wheelchairs and hospital beds—all of those things have to be totaled up. The economist comes in and puts a price tag on the plan and tells us—and ultimately will tell a jury—what a reasonable amount of money will be to compensate that client for those actual losses and those future losses.

These are the kinds of experts you need in a trucking collision case: accident reconstruction, a trucking expert, a life care planner, a vocational expert, and probably also a *psychologist* or *psychiatrist* because people who have been involved in these collisions often struggle with PTSD. That's a very common thing that we see in our practice. These collisions are so traumatic and so severe that people have nightmares and relive them for months, if not years, afterward.

I often find that people are sad and depressed and anxious about their experience, and then they're embarrassed to tell anybody. This is common, and I tell all of my clients this is common. I want them to seek the help they need to get through this trauma. That often means a psychologist or psychiatrist is needed to help with the emotional side of things.

In cases where someone has lost a loved one, we've also used *grief experts*. That's especially important if they've lost a child. Parents aren't supposed to outlive their children. The grief of these parents, or the grief of husbands or wives who've lost a spouse, can be paralyzing. That's another reason the psychologist or psychiatrist is important in these cases.

There are experts that we use who explain to the jury about the types of grief that people experience and the cycle of grief, in which they go from being angry to feeling guilty to being incredibly sad to depressed to anxious and back again. That's an important part of this, having an expert evaluate the client because all of those things are damages. All of those things are injuries. And all of those items go into the decision of a jury as to what will fully and fairly compensate the client.

Our expert witnesses on all of these fronts help explain to a jury what the client is experiencing so that the jury can then decide what will fully and fairly compensate the client.

Class

As I said at the beginning of this chapter, a trucking case is not like the typical rear-ender in front of the convenience store. It's in a different class because the stakes are so high. Most of these cases involve millions of dollars. There's no such thing as a small trucking collision. No one just shakes it off and walks away. Typically in a trucking case someone is severely injured, permanently injured, disabled, or even killed. There are millions of dollars at stake, maybe even tens of millions. The insurance company and the trucking company know that.

The lawyer who's representing the injured party needs to know that as well. He or she needs to be prepared to fight for as long as the fight takes. They're not going to pay millions of dollars willingly. They're not going to pay millions of dollars just because the lawyer writes a couple of letters. To get what the client deserves in these types of cases, you're going to have to hire the experts. You're going to have to file the lawsuit. You're going to have to take the depositions. You're going to have to go to court. You're going to have to fight and claw, because insurance companies don't make billions of dollars a year by just giving money away. They don't make billions of dollars a year by giving up easily.

They make billions of dollars a year by fighting to the end and by paying as little as they possibly can. My job is to get the insurance company to fully and fairly compensate the injured party. If that takes six months, great. If that takes three years, that's okay as well.

Chapter 2

Commercial Motor Vehicles Are Everywhere

The title of this chapter might seem to be overstating the obvious. We all know that commercial motor vehicles—trucks—are everywhere. We all see those 18-wheelers, one after another after another, on the road all the time, right? Everyone understands that the 18-wheeler on the interstate is a commercial motor vehicle. And of course it is; there's no question about that. Because it's a commercial motor vehicle (CMV), it is regulated by the Federal Motor Carrier Safety Administration.

This is what you need to know: While it is obvious that an 18-wheeler is a commercial motor vehicle, what's not so obvious is that there are many more commercial motor vehicles around us every day, in every circumstance, and every part of our lives. It might be a Ford F-250 pickup truck hauling workers to a natural gas well site. It might be a tow truck. It might be a school bus. It might be a snowplow. All of these are commercial motor vehicles, or can be.

These are just a few examples of commercial motor vehicles:

Semi

Pickup

Water truck

Box truck

Pickup towing

Large pickup with dumper

So while the Ford F-250 pickup, or the Dodge 3500 Ram, or the 3500 or 4500 Silverado might not look like a typical commercial motor vehicle, it may well be depending on the circumstances. Depending on who owns the vehicle, depending on what they're hauling, depending on the nature of the work that the truck and the people in it are doing, that truck may well qualify as a commercial motor vehicle.

It's crucial to know the difference between a commercial motor vehicle and a regular personal vehicle. The reason is that certain rules apply to a CMV, through the Federal Motor Carrier Safety Administration, that will not apply to a personal vehicle. The CMV is required to have a higher standard of care. The motor carrier—the owner of the CMV—is required to comply with a whole set of rules and regulations specific to CMVs.

In the previous chapter we discussed why you need an expert in trucking cases. This is one of the key reasons. You need to hire a lawyer who understands the difference between a commercial motor vehicle and a personal vehicle. That means understanding not only the specific rules and regulations that apply, but also recognizing the significantly higher financial stakes.

CMVs are required to carry much higher levels of insurance than personal vehicles. For example, a CMV is required to carry a minimum of $750,000 of insurance. That is a federal requirement. Personal vehicle insurance requirements vary from state to state, but minimum coverage is typically in the range of just $25,000. So the huge difference in dollar value makes these cases much more challenging.

Having that minimum of $750,000 on the line in these incidents takes everything to another level entirely. It brings out a whole new level of investigation by the motor carrier. It brings in a much different class of defense attorney to defend the motor carrier. We're talking a whole new level of everything in this circumstance. If it were only $25,000 at stake, the company would farm the case out to some local defense firm. They would pay the $25,000 and that would be the end of it.

But when you're talking $750,000, or a million, or five million, or ten million dollars in coverage, the stakes are higher for everybody. That's why the investigation needs to be so much more involved and you have to have a law firm that focuses on tractor trailer cases because the trucking companies and their insurance companies will have defense attorneys and investigators whose sole focus is defending tractor trailer and commercial motor vehicle accidents. If you have the misfortune to be involved in one of these cases, you need a law firm that will protect your interests, and your rights, and your family. That law firm needs to focus on commercial motor vehicles, how to prosecute those cases, and how to make sure that the case is handled appropriately.

The bottom line here is that if you or your family members have been injured—or if a family member has been killed— by *any* kind of truck, you can't take for granted that it is just somebody's farm truck and that it's going to be a run-of-the-mill case. Call in the experts right away to investigate and determine whether in fact you have a commercial motor vehicle case. Because if you do, you will be dealing with a completely different set of rules and regulations.

Chapter 3

Trucks Are Held to a Higher Standard

We've talked previously in this book about the Federal Motor Carrier Safety Administration (FMCSA). The Federal Motor Carrier Safety Administration publishes a detailed handbook of rules and regulations—the Federal Motor Carrier Safety Regulations, or FMCSR—that govern every aspect of trucking operations, from the trucking company, to the driver, and to the vehicle itself. It's essentially the Bible of trucking. The ultimate purpose of the FMCSR is to ensure safety in trucking operations. These rules are to protect the public, to protect the driver of the commercial motor vehicle, and to protect the motor carrier who owns the truck and is paying to put this truck on the highway. The primary goal of the Federal Motor Carrier Safety Administration is safety for all.

Driving a commercial motor vehicle is considered a "safety-sensitive" job. It's not like running to the store to grab a gallon of milk. The primary responsibility of a CMV operator is to drive heavy-duty trucks on the public highway. When your job is to drive these heavy-duty 18-wheelers, tractor trailers, Ford F-250s, Dodge Ram 4500s, and all of these other buses and vans—when your entire job day-in and day-out is to be on the highway driving these vehicles—you are considered to have a safety-sensitive duty, and because you have that safety-sensitive duty, there are going to be very specific rules and regulations that will apply to you.

The driver of a commercial motor vehicle is held to a higher standard. It's like the difference between a forklift driver and a

Segway driver. The forklift driver must adhere to more regulations than a Segway driver. Why? Because there is more danger inherent in operating a forklift than there is in operating a Segway. It's the same with commercial motor vehicles versus personal motor vehicles. Just as there are certain certifications and tests that people have to pass before they're allowed to drive and operate a forklift, there are certain tests that operators of commercial motor vehicles are required to take. Their employer has to accompany them and make sure that they are able to pass these tests and operate the vehicle in a safe fashion before they put these drivers out on the road. The employer is supposed to document all of that. Drivers need to be properly trained, and they need to have that training updated from time to time.

Before the driver even gets into the truck or into the CMV, the motor carrier that owns the vehicle has a primary obligation to make sure that he or she, the person they are putting behind the wheel, is qualified to drive the vehicle in question. The driver *must* be qualified to drive the truck, or the van, or the tow truck, or the Ford F-250, or the tractor trailer. And the Federal Motor Carrier Safety Regulations are very specific about what a motor carrier has to do to determine whether or not the driver is qualified. We talked about this in Chapter One, in relation to the Donna Collins case. To reiterate briefly, the motor carrier is required to have on file the driver's employment history, residential history, criminal history, and driving record. Where do they live? Who have they worked for? What traffic citations have they had? Have they ever had their license suspended, revoked, or disciplined in a fashion, and if so, why?

The motor carrier has a whole laundry list of requirements regarding driver qualifications. This is not optional. It's not, well, we'll do it when we get around to it. The carrier is obligated to obtain and document all of this information to make sure that the driver is qualified. All of that happens before the driver even gets into the truck.

Once the driver's qualifications have been established, FMCSA has still more rules and regulations that govern the driver's work, such as how long the driver of a truck can work and drive in a 24-hour day. For example, the FMCSR states that a driver cannot work and operate a CMV more than 14 hours in one day. That seems clear, doesn't it? But the truth is that there are motor carriers out there that routinely require their employees to work and drive 15, 18, 20, sometimes even more than 20 hours a day, on a regular basis.

What happens when the motor carrier and its drivers fail to adhere to these workday standards? Let me tell you another war story.

Energy Services

You are going to think that I made this story up, but I promise you that it is 110 percent true. The commercial motor vehicle in this case was a natural gas service truck. It was a Ford F250 pickup truck, and as in the Donna Collins case, the truck was pulling a 20-foot steel trailer. The truck was owned by another containment company.

In this case, the truck's crew of four guys had traveled from Anmoore, West Virginia to Ohio. They left at 4:00 a.m. from the shop in Anmoore, West Virginia and went to their work site in Ohio, a trip of two and a half to three hours.

When they left the yard in Anmoore, their boss, whose nickname was Shorty (you can't make this up), was there, so he knew that they had set out at 4:00 a.m. Shorty was not only their boss, he was also a co-owner of the company. The crew drove to Ohio, where they worked all day and in to the late evening. They called Shorty from the job site between 10:00 p.m. and 10:30 p.m. and told him that they had finally finished the work. He said okay, boys, come on back. They left the site around 10:30 p.m. to return from Ohio to Anmoore, West Virginia.

Remember what I said earlier: The Federal Motor Carrier Safety Administration says that a driver can only work and drive 14 hours in one day. Once you hit that 14-hour mark, you can no longer drive a vehicle. You have to stop, get a hotel, and stay where you are. You're not allowed to drive.

They almost made it. They were ten minutes from the shop in Anmoore when the driver fell asleep and crashed the truck into a pole on the interstate. He had been working or driving for 22 consecutive hours.

My client in this case was the family of a 26-year-old man who had been sitting in the rear seat of this Ford F250 pickup truck. He was killed immediately when the truck hit this pole.

The Federal Motor Carrier Safety Administration requires that truck drivers keep what's called a driver's daily log. This log keeps track of the driver's entire day. It documents where he was driving, how long he was driving, when he went through a weight station, or when he was pulled over. Because the driver is operating a commercial motor vehicle, everything that he does throughout the day must be documented, and the number of hours driven is tracked.

Obviously they couldn't document a 22-hour day, so the driver put phony information into the daily log to suggest that he had worked and driven not 22 hours, but more like 8 or 10 hours. He was obviously in violation; he knew it and everybody else knew it. Remember, there were four people in the truck. One of the men who survived, another passenger, was a very close friend of the guy who had died.

The victim's family hired us immediately after the accident. That was another key to this. Because we were hired so quickly after the accident, I was able to interview these people within days of this terrible collision.

That meant that I interviewed the best friend of the guy who was killed. His name was Kenny Schindler. Kenny was a very good guy, a hardworking young man, about 25 or 26 years old. We were at Panera Bread and I'll remember this interview as long as I live. Kenny was with his girlfriend and we sat out on the porch. I said "Kenny, tell me what happened." He told me the whole story. He told me that they had worked or driven 22 straight hours and that Shorty knew that. Shorty was the one who had told them to phony up the driver's daily log. That sounded great for our case, but I was curious and worried—suspicious might be the better word. This guy was kind of the leader of that four-man crew, and I wondered if he was just trying to cover his tracks.

But Kenny had more to say. He told me that they had not only put phony information into the driver's daily logs for that day, but they routinely did that at Shorty's direction because the company didn't have enough drivers. The company's story began to unravel. As I interviewed more and more current and former employees, they all told me exactly the same thing. What gave it away was that these guys were reporting that they were resting in a sleeper berth. On a tractor trailer, that's the place where the guys can sleep in the back. But these Ford F250s obviously don't have a sleeper berth. They were just making stuff up.

We had dozens and dozens of examples of driver's daily logs that were all full of phony information. Some of these employees and former employees couldn't wait to tell the story about what was going on at this company. They'd been driving 16, 18, or 20 hours on a regular basis because the company didn't have enough employees or enough drivers. Shorty was telling them to do this.

So we started looking into the company a little bit. This company was called Energy Services, and it was an outfit out of Grand Junction, Colorado. When we looked into the history of Energy Services, we discovered that they'd had so many violations of the Federal Motor Carrier rules and regulations that their Department of Transportation (DOT) license had been revoked.

I couldn't understand how they were operating this truck. Then I figured it out. The owners of Energy Services, who had lost their DOT license, started a new company called Energy Specialties. Same owners. They applied for—and got—a Department of Transportation license and DOT number and then gave it to Energy Services so that they could keep working. In trucking terminology it is referred to as a chameleon company. Like a chameleon, it's the same animal, meaning for all practical purposes it's the same company. It might be a different color, or have a different name, but it's the same company.

Energy Specialties basically defrauded the Department of Transportation to get a DOT number to replace the one that they had lost through an identical company (Energy Services). They got this DOT number so they could keep working. They just started the whole thing again. Energy Specialties had no employees. No customers. No accounts receivable. No insurance. No property. No assets, nothing. It was just a shell company. It was a shell company formed only to get the DOT license, so that Energy Services could go back to doing whatever they wanted to do. The settlement in that case is confidential.

One might be tempted to say that this is an isolated incident, but it is not. This is an epidemic, and I'll tell you why. It's because the theme is money. Profit over safety is the theme of all of these companies. They're not worried about protecting the public. They're not even worried about the safety of their own employees. They're worried about making as many trips, taking as many loads, and doing as much work as they can, so they can make as much money as they can.

Their hope is that no one gets hurt. But unfortunately people are being hurt-very badly. The reality is this: Tractor trailer companies, for example, and their drivers, get paid by the load. The more loads they take, the more cargo they transport. The more trips they make, the more money they make.

If a truck is pulled to the side because the brakes are bad or it's not operating properly, they're losing money. It's the same with these natural gas service companies. If they don't get these guys out into the field, to put up the tarps, lay down the plastic, and do all the work that they are required to do, they're not making any money.

Look at this Energy Services case I just described. If the crew had spent the night in Ohio, as they should have done since they had already timed out, they would not have been able to go out to another well site the next morning. They would have been driving home, because they had no more supplies or equipment. They would have lost a day of work. That's why Shorty wanted them back.

But if the crew had followed the rules and spent the night in Ohio, maybe the victim killed in the collision would be alive today.

These guys at Energy Services would tell me how they would circumvent the weigh stations so that they didn't have to show their drivers' logs to the DOT officials. The company instructed them to do that. These drivers are just 25- or 26-year-old guys. They have no agenda. They get paid by the hour, whether they spend the night in Ohio or whether they drive all the way home. They don't care. It's the company that is giving them these instructions, because it is the company that is incentivized to break the rules.

Understanding the rules can make your case

The trucking industry is a very complicated industry. What makes it complicated is that it involves much more than just operating a truck or jumping into the cab of a truck and driving it from one place to another. It involves loading the truck. It involves maintaining the truck. It involves making sure the truck driver is qualified. It involves making sure that the truck driver is trained. It involves making sure that the truck driver adheres to the rules and regulations of the road, and that includes not encouraging drivers to break the rules or giving them incentives to break the rules.

The FMCSR, as I said earlier, is the Bible for this industry. It is what the motor carriers and the drivers are expected to be trained on and what they're expected to abide by. It leaves very little wiggle room. When the regulations say x, they're supposed to do x. When the regulations say that they're supposed to document information and maintain that documentation, they're required by law to do so. It's not an option. These rules and regulations are in place to protect the public, to protect the driver, and to protect the motor carrier. It is all based upon safety.

Some of these things are intricate. For example, it's like the Lord giveth and the Lord taketh away. There will be a big global rule saying, "Don't do x," and then it will add, "Except when . . ." followed by a dozen "except whens." It can be a very complicated process trying to identify the applicable rule versus the basic rule.

For example, consider the 14-hour rule that was so important in this Energy Services case. It would seem very simple to say, well, did the guy work and drive more than 14 hours a day in one 24-hour period? The answer is either yes or no. But while the rule seems very simple, there are many, many exceptions to it. Those exceptions are complicated; they depend on how far the driver is driving and what kind of work they're doing. That seemingly simple rule has a number of convoluted exceptions.

Then the next question becomes, do any of the exceptions apply? Which ones? There are so many of these exceptions. That's why you need a law firm that knows those rules and knows those exceptions, and knows what does apply and what does not apply. It is much more difficult and complicated than it might seem.

The *FMCSA Handbook* sets the standard. In my experience, however, the companies very seldom abide by all of these rules. That does help the plaintiffs because there are so many rules and regulations that these trucking companies are expected to abide by. The companies are incentivized by the economics of the trucking industry. They are incentivized to break these rules, to ignore these rules, and to skirt these rules. The economic incentive for them is to keep the trucks on the road for as long as possible because the more loads they haul, the more distance they go, the more people they have out in the field, the more money they are making.

If the company has to leave a truck behind because the brakes are bad, that's going to cost them money, and they don't want to do that. If they have a driver who's not really qualified but he's close and they need to get guys out into the field, then close is going to be good enough for them. Close is not good enough for the public, and close is not good enough for the Federal Motor Carrier Safety Administration. That's what happens time and time again. When the truck driver has worked and driven his 14 hours and he needs to stop and stay at a hotel, the trucking company doesn't want to pay for that hotel because usually it's not just one hotel room. It's three or four hotel rooms because the driver has a crew with him. If that truck driver doesn't get home with that crew that night, they can't send them back out the next day, or they'll be late. Again, that costs them money.

Because those trucking companies routinely ignore the rules, skirt the rules, and don't completely follow the rules, people get hurt. No one ever thinks that the truck driver's going to fall asleep. No one ever thinks that the truck isn't going to get stopped. No one ever thinks that, "Well, this guy's qualified enough. He's probably okay." It's going to be that one time when he's not okay, or when a driver does fall asleep, that people get injured, often severely injured, and maybe even killed. It only takes that one time to alter the course of someone's life forever. That's why these rules are in place, and that's why these rules can be so important to a plaintiff's case. It is essential to make sure that the trucking company has abided by its requirements in operating its commercial motor vehicles. The FMCSR provides the standard; in the case of a trucking collision, the plaintiff's lawyer will measure the actions of the trucking company and the driver against this standard. That's why it is so important for a plaintiff in one of these cases to be represented by a firm with a thorough understanding of the FMCSA regulations.

When is a truck not a CMV?

For most people, a truck is just a truck, whether it's an 18-wheeler or a run-of-the-mill pickup truck. But when that truck is involved in a collision, the distinction becomes critical, and frankly, it's for the lawyer to determine whether the truck in question is a commercial motor vehicle. A CMV typically has a Department of Transportation (DOT) number on the side of it, which generally gives it away as a commercial motor vehicle. But there's a caveat: Some companies allow their employees to take these trucks home with them at the end of the work day.

For example, many of these natural gas well companies allow their employees to use these trucks as their mode of transportation to and from the field. So at the end of the day they'll take these trucks home. Well, suppose it's Saturday morning, and the guy's running to the store to get something, and he is in an accident. Under those circumstances, will the truck be considered a CMV or is it going to be considered a personal motor vehicle? That's not a simple question. The answer will depend on many circumstances, and it will be up to the lawyer to figure out whether the truck is truly a commercial motor vehicle in this instance. Our goal in these cases is always to bring it under the umbrella of a CMV, but only if the facts support that conclusion.

Chapter 4

Trucking Companies are Faster than You

There's no getting around this one. The truth is that the trucking company will always be faster than you are. Trucking companies, particularly the major trucking companies, have crash teams—what they call "go teams"—all over the country. When there's a crash or a collision involving a tractor trailer or other commercial motor vehicle, many of these trucking companies and their insurance companies are able to send people out to the crash scene within minutes of being notified of the crash.

Think about how this happens. Suppose a tractor trailer is involved in a catastrophic collision on the interstate.

As soon as the collision happens, that truck driver, out on the interstate, is on the phone with his dispatcher right away telling the dispatcher what has happened. The dispatcher reports the incident to management, management talks to the lawyer or to their insurance company, and they immediately dispatch lawyers and investigators to the site, often within an hour of a collision. They have people all over the country who do this. Often while the state troopers are there, or even while the EMS are still there on the scene, they have their investigators and their lawyers out there measuring skid marks, taking statements, taking photographs, and taking video at the scene of the collision. Before the troopers even leave the scene of the accident, before the trucks are towed away, the company is already preparing a defense in the case.

What does that mean for the victim? It's important for people who are involved in a collision with a truck, or their family, to contact an attorney as quickly as possible. The common myth is that you need to get a lawyer within the first week. *The reality is that a week is much too long to wait.* Time is of the essence, especially if the collision is on an interstate highway. Here in West Virginia and Ohio, we have I-79, I-70, I-77, I 71, I 270 US Route 50, and US Route 33. People are passing through the states of West Virginia and Ohio 24 hours a day. Those drivers are not all local people. They may have witnessed an accident but they're on their way to Kentucky, or to Georgia, or to Minnesota, or wherever. Sometimes the police don't even have a chance to speak to them. Now we're going to have to track them down and sometimes it gets hard. Memories fade with time and people don't want to cooperate.

The physical evidence also gets lost over time. In inclement weather, rain or snow washes away the skid marks.

The law enforcement authorities do a great job of investigating these cases, but once they're finished with the immediate accident scene, they're often called away to another collision, or some other criminal activity. That means their attention is not always focused on the collision at hand. As the plaintiff's lawyers, we want to get our own investigators out there right away. We want to get our accident reconstruction experts on scene. We want to take our own statements, and measure our own skid marks, and take our own photographs, and take our own video so that we can start building our case. Law enforcement is good—they do a great job here—but we want to help them.

In some instances we are able to assist the law enforcement investigation. In a case I'm working on right now, we became part of the deputy sheriff's investigation because we had the ability, through our expert witnesses, to download the computer data from the tractor trailer. They did not, so we shared our data with them to assist law enforcement with their investigation. That was only possible because we were on that case immediately. There was a fatality, and the family called us shortly after the collision. The family just needed questions answered. They were obviously grieving for the unexpected loss of a loved one, and they needed someone to stand for them in this terrible time. They didn't know where to turn. Fortunately, they turned to us so we were able to get our experts on the scene figuring out what happened. We were evaluating the tractor trailer, evaluating our clients car, down loading computer data from both vehicles and collecting evidence at the scene. We were meeting with law enforcement and finding out what they have had done in their investigation and what still needed to be done. As I said, our investigation allowed law enforcement to do their job as well. We were very happy to be of assistance with that.

I can't overstate how quickly these trucking companies and insurance companies mobilize in the event of a collision. I have seen truck drivers who have been fired on the scene. I've seen it happen twice: The lawyer for the trucking company met the truck driver at the scene of the collision, relieved him of his duties, took him to a hotel, and left him to find his own way home. Most of these truck drivers are from out of state. They were fired right at the scene of the accident. As I said, the lawyers go right to the scene.

A normal run-of-the-mill plaintiff's lawyer, who has a general practice, might do a few car accidents, a couple motorcycle accidents, maybe a divorce, and other types of cases. In a trucking case like the ones I've described, that general practice lawyer is typically out-gunned right away because they don't know what to do and how quickly it needs to be done. They don't have the expert witnesses immediately available to them to meet them at the scene. They don't have experts who can come at a moment's notice to start the reconstruction process. In our practice, we get referrals all the time from other lawyers, which we appreciate. These are lawyers who realize that we have a practice that focuses on trucking accidents and they get us involved in their cases, which is a good thing. It's important that the person injured or the family of the person who was injured or killed gets us involved in the case immediately.

Let me just be blunt about it. This is what we do. This is what my trial team is prepared to do. This is what they're trained to do. This is what we do on a regular basis. You do not want me to represent you in a divorce. But you do want us to represent in a trucking case.

Our clients will tell you all you need to know about our response and our ability to handle these cases. Just look at the reviews on our Google listing.

Let's face it. In these cases, you're going up against national trucking companies. You're going up against some of the largest insurance carriers in the world. They have the resources, the sophistication, and the experience to handle these cases. People who are involved, or who have been injured, in a trucking case need—and deserve—to have that same kind of expertise and experience on their side.

The insurance company will act like they're trying to help you. They will act like they're looking out for your best interest, but they are not. Their interest is to pay as little as possible. Our job is to protect the interest of our client, to answer the client's questions about how and why this happened, and to make sure that the client is adequately and fairly compensated. That's our job and that's why people hire us.

The best advice I can give is call an attorney ASAP. In the Donna Collins case that I described in the Introduction, the family called us the day after the accident, which was appropriate timing. This woman was in a life-threatening situation, and so they had to fly her from the local hospital to the trauma center. Once she got to the trauma center it was late in the evening. The family called us the next morning. I didn't know anything about the case at that point but I knew it was bad. I knew this family and I knew it was bad.

When they called me, I was out of town. I was in Cleveland, Ohio at a conference where I was speaking, believe it or not, on trucking cases. When I hung up the phone with the Collins family, I left Cleveland and drove straight to Ruby Memorial Hospital that same afternoon because I knew these people needed us. From my car, on my way from Cleveland to Ruby Memorial Hospital, I called our reconstruction expert. He was on his way the next day from Charlotte, North Carolina to get that accident scene reconstructed. We were out there right away taking statements and photographing the vehicles.

Preserving the evidence

One of the most important reasons for getting on the case immediately is to preserve the evidence.

Of course, there will be some evidence that is outside of our control and other evidence that is within our control. The most important evidence within our control is going to be our client's car. In almost every circumstance, our client's car will have the "black box." The black box is really an electronic computer module (ECM) that records all kinds of very important information. The ECM will give us a great deal of information about how fast our client was going, or when he or she hit the brakes. It can give us all kinds of information that will help us reconstruct the accident. So we have that vehicle, but we need to make sure that we put a hold on the vehicle immediately because the insurance company that was insuring the client will want to get rid of it.

If the vehicle is totaled, they'll want to move it to a salvage yard. The car will get salvaged, and everything will be destroyed including the ECM. We need to preserve that vehicle as evidence by contacting the insurance company and saying, "Hold that car.

We do not want that car sold, altered, or destroyed. We want to be able to inspect it. The defense, the trucking company, has a right to inspect it. We don't want any evidence lost." We can control that and if we tell them to hold it, they are going to be required to hold that vehicle until we say it's okay to let it go. But if we don't let them know, they may get rid of it, and then that evidence is lost.

The evidence that we can't control is the truck that was involved in the collision. Most often the company wants to get that truck back out on the road as quickly as possible, because if that truck's sitting in a tow yard or maintenance building, it's not making them any money. From my perspective, I don't want that truck touched, or altered, or changed, or repaired until my experts have an opportunity to photograph it, take video of it, and download all of its computer data. The computer data from the truck, just like the computer data from my client's car, is going to be very important in reconstructing this collision so that we can determine why the collision occurred and who was at fault.

The photographs of the truck, the physical evidence from the truck, and the video recording of the truck will all be important in reconstructing what happened.

Advances in technology are helping us in this effort. We are now using drones in accident reconstruction. We use drones to videotape the vehicles involved so that we can do 3-D animation of how the accident occurred. We are using drones at the scene of the accident so that we can get perfect measurements—exact measurements—of intersections, of highways, of interstates. Also, trucks often times have electronic tracking devices such as GPS units or other commercially available tracking devices. These devices allow us to determine the route a truck has taken, when and how often it stopped or how fast it was going at certain points in time. Also, when comparing the GPS information to a truck driver's phone records you may very well be able to determine if the driver was using his or her cell phone while operating the truck in violation of state and federal law. You can now see how important it is for us to thoroughly inspect the truck-inside and out.

Just as we want our client's car preserved for evidence, we want to make sure that the trucking company preserves the truck in the state it was in at the time of the collision. We want to gather as much information as we can to reconstruct the collision because that's going to be important in the investigation of this case.

There will be other evidence that's out of our control. It might be the skid marks on the highway or at the intersection. It might be the debris that's left behind from a collision, glass and a hubcap or whatever it might be. Often, that physical evidence can be very important in reconstructing the case, so it's important where that evidence winds up.

If it's two, three, or four weeks down the line, who knows where that debris might end up? It could get cleaned up by the Department of Highways. It could be lost, it could be blown over a hill, it could just disintegrate in some fashion. We want to get out to the scene of the accident as soon as we can. We have some evidence within our control, but there will be a lot of evidence that is not in our control. We want to make sure that the evidence that is not within our control is preserved and handled appropriately.

Chapter 5

Your Word is Not Enough

A thousand words ... or much more

It's a cliché but it's true: A picture is worth a thousand words. That's always true in preparing these cases. What's also true is that a moving picture—a video recording—is worth even more. Often we buy our clients a video camera so they can record everything in video and in still photos. These days the typical digital camera that you buy at your local electronics store also shoots video. It's worth it to us to buy these video cameras because we want the clients or their family members to photograph and make video recordings of the patient's injuries and progress. Most people these days understand the importance of photographs from the scene of a collision—the vehicles, the damage, the site itself—but many fail to realize how important the photos of the aftermath are. We want a visual record of bruises and surgical incisions and burns and stitches and broken bones. All of that needs to be photographed and video recorded.

I understand that this may sound coarse, or grotesque, or maybe even inflammatory. But it's vitally important. Patients injured in these collisions are entitled to be compensated for those injuries. In trucking collisions the injuries are seldom minor ones. If the client suffered a broken femur and needed surgery on their leg, if they had to have rods and screws and plates put in their leg, which they'll have forever, they're entitled to be compensated for that. Maybe they have been left with a great big scar down the middle of their thigh from where the surgeons had to go in and insert those rods and screws and plates, and then maybe clean out an infection, and perform other treatments. Maybe they have needed physical and or occupational therapy. The jury is entitled to know everything that the client went through.

What makes this visual record so important? Here's another familiar saying: Time heals all wounds. That one is true, too. Bruises fade. Broken bones mend. Surgical scars heal. But none of that healing happens overnight. It can be a long and painful process, and it can leave lasting effects. The visual record of photographs and video serves to document that whole long healing process and all that the client has gone through. These people had to live through that. They just didn't wake up after surgery with the wound looking like it does at a trial three years later. They may have gone months and months with a wound vac and an infection and debridement surgeries and all of those kinds of things to get to that place three years later where it doesn't look too bad. I want the jury to see what my client has endured to get to that three-year mark because they're entitled to be compensated for every day of that.

Jimmy's story

Let me give you an example of how this visual record made a huge difference in a case. My client was a 7-year-old boy—let's call him Jimmy—who had been severely burned. His were probably the most horrific burns I've ever seen. He was burned on over 68 percent of his body.

I didn't know the family at all before the case, and when they first contacted me, I wasn't even entirely sure what the case was about. I knew it was bad, though, and I went to meet the family at the West Penn Burn Center in Pittsburgh, Pennsylvania. The family didn't know me and I didn't know them, but on my way to the burn center, I stopped and bought them a video camera. When I got there I told the parents, "Look, I don't know yet if you have a case, but we're going to look into it. In the meantime, I want you to record on video everything that your son goes through, from the debridement surgeries, to the washings, to the wound care, to the dressing changes, to the physical therapy."

That video became one of the cornerstones in getting a significant settlement for Jimmy. If the judge were going to allow the jury to see the dressing changes and the wounds and the physical therapy and just trying to teach this boy how to walk again, it would have been just devastating to the defendants. What was most devastating, and I'll never forget it, were the cries and the screams. It was not only the video, but also the audio. This was real life, and it was the definition of suffering.

We use the term "pain and suffering" all the time, but this recording was so much more. It expressed the very essence of suffering. No one who heard it could ever get past it, and it made a huge difference in that case. Without it, there would have been pictures of a boy who had serious scars, but that would not have done him justice. Let me say it this way: It would not have done justice to Jimmy and his family for what they really went through. It was incredible what this 7-year-old child had to endure just to survive.

Confidentiality prevents me from disclosing any details, but I can say this: Because we had those recordings, the case resulted in a significant settlement with several major national corporations, some of the biggest in the country.

As an aside, I should point out that our firm routinely takes on some of the biggest corporations and insurance companies in the country. When you decide to take on an AIG or a Liberty Mutual or a State Farm, you need to realize just how big these companies are. They have more money than they know what to do with. If they want to outspend you, they can and they will. If they choose to do so, they can get five different law firms to make you run around spending time and money. If they decide to see if they can wear you down, they will. Those kinds of insurance companies and those kinds of corporations will do anything and everything they have to do to save themselves money.

It's common in trucking cases to be dealing with some of the biggest corporations in the country. And they are insured by the biggest insurance companies in the country and sometimes in the world. That can be intimidating. Any firm that is going to take them on has to have the financial wherewithal and experience to stand up to them. Frankly, the plaintiff's lawyer has to have the resources—and the courage—to be able to say, "Okay, I'm ready. Let's go. Let's saddle up and let's see what you've got." There are a lot of people who wouldn't want to take on that responsibility and they shouldn't. Our firm, though, regularly takes on these giant corporations. We have the resources and the experience and WE ARE NOT AFRAID.

That's one of the key differences between our firm and other law firms. For example, I wouldn't want to get involved in a divorce. That is not what I do and I don't want to do it. That might be two local lawyers, who have known each other all their lives, sparring over who gets the 401K. There's a place for that, and there's certainly a need for that, but that's outside of what we do. That's not my expertise or interest. I'm accustomed to taking on Walmart and State Farm and AIG. That doesn't bother me at all. Bring them on!

Witness statements

It's not only the victim who should be recorded. It's also extremely helpful to have recorded statements from any witnesses to the collision.

Recorded statements are very important in our work. The sooner we can take that statement, the better off we are. When you take someone's recorded statement within a day or two of the accident, it typically still carries all of the emotion of the accident. All of the feelings, reactions, and details are still fresh and close to the surface. Such a statement will often be more enlightening for the case. It will help us build our case, give us more information, and will typically be more complete because the event was so recent. Time has not yet faded the person's memory.

With the passage of time, all of us will forget details. The immediate emotion will fade, and the retelling will become more matter-of-fact. Once that happens, details often get lost.

In Chapter Three, I described our Energy Services case, where a young man—his name was Timmy Roth—was killed when the driver of the truck in which he was riding fell asleep at the wheel after working 22 consecutive hours and crashed his truck on the interstate.

One of the most important pieces of our case was the recorded statement of Kenny Schindler. He was one of Timmy Roth's best friends, and he was a passenger in the front seat of the truck when the collision happened.

I took Kenny Schindler's statement just days after the accident. It was a very emotional time for him; he had just lost his best friend and colleague in that accident. His emotion brought us truth. His emotion brought us completeness. His emotion brought us powerful testimony: the facts that eventually condemned the company. This young man told us how they had worked and driven 22 straight hours. He told us how the co-owner of the company instructed them to commit fraud and falsify the information on the driver's daily report, to try to hide the fact that they had worked and driven for 22 straight hours. He told us how the owner of the company had instructed them to do that many, many times prior to this instance.

I believe that it was the fact that we were able to talk to Kenny so soon after the accident that allowed us to obtain the important information that proved so devastating to the company. If we had talked with him two or three months later, I'm not entirely sure that we would have gotten that information because the emotion of it would have faded a bit. He might have been a bit more stoic; he might have been a little more guarded in what he was willing to tell us.

When I'm talking with a witness like Kenny Schindler, I don't want him to forget that night. As he was telling me the story, you could see the collision in his eyes, because it was so fresh. Six months later, I'm not sure it would have been that fresh in his mind, and the statement we got might have been very different.

Because we spoke with him early, he was completely unguarded, forthright, and truthful with us. The information he gave us was so key to the case. When I walked away from him that afternoon of our interview, I knew that the company was done. The company was done and there was nothing they could do about it, because it had all been recorded. When I met with Kenny, I took out my iPhone and I asked him if I had his permission to record our conversation. When he agreed, I turned on my recorder. I confirmed on the recording that he knew I was recording the conversation and that I had his permission. I explained to him whom I represented, which he understood, and he told me everything I needed to know about the case.

I had the recording transcribed and typed up. Then I sent it back to him to read, to make any corrections he thought were appropriate and he signed the statement verifying its accuracy. This is what we try to do in every case. It's extremely important, and another way of preserving vital evidence.

Technological advances

I've been working on trucking cases for many years, and I can tell you that today's technology has opened up amazing possibilities for us in building these cases.

For example, today we are able to use drone technology in a number of ways, both in the pretrial phase and the trial phase of a case.

We use drones in accident reconstruction, and also for measuring purposes. We can utilize computer data to tell us far exactly it is from the stop light to where the car was at a given time.

If we want to know the distance at an accident scene—how far it is from point A to point B—we use two different things. It may surprise you to learn that the first thing we do is use Google Maps. That gives us a lot of excellent, accurate information. Google Maps tells you when its photograph were taken, it gives you different perspectives and different views, including overhead views and street views, and it also has a way to measure distance. You can put point A on the map, add point B, and it will give you the exact distance.

Along with Google Maps, we use drones at the scenes of these accidents so that we can give the jury and the judge a good overview and perspective of the scene. Many of these accidents occur at intersections, and sometimes these are very complicated intersections. There may well be multiple lanes coming from different directions. A good overhead video will help a judge and jury understand how the accident occurred. The video also helps us with measurements and gives us information concerning where other traffic might be at certain distances from an intersection.

The drones are small and simple to use. The operator just pops it out of its case and seconds later it's in the air. The drone has a couple of different GoPro cameras attached to it, and the Go Pros transmit to a monitor on the ground that allows the operator to see the view that the drone is seeing. On the monitor, you can see what the drone is seeing and you can make sure you're getting the views that you want to get.

We also use drones to create animations. Remember that I said a picture is worth a thousand words? A good animation will help us show a judge and a jury exactly how the collision occurred. I'm working on a case right now where a vehicle crossed the median of an intersection and crashed into a truck. We represent the occupants of the truck. It was a Freightliner tractor trailer that crashed into the occupants of the truck and smashed into the tractor trailer which burst into flames. We're using an animation to describe to the judge and to the jury how this collision occurred, who was at fault and what could have been done to avoid this horrible collision.

Drones have become extremely important to us these days, and they help us with mediations. We're in the business of trying to get cases settled for the clients, but at the same time we want to be prepared to go to trial. We use all of these technological developments—drones and Google Maps and animations—so that we can explain to the defendant and their insurance company why the trucking company owes the money. These tools help us in trying to convince them and persuade them to pay what's fair and reasonable to a client who has been injured or to the family of someone who has been killed.

Chapter 6

You Need More Experts

By now it should be clear that experts are invaluable at every stage of building a case in the wake of a trucking collision. You need expert testimony.

It starts right away with the accident reconstructionist. That's the expert we want on the scene as soon as possible after the incident. As we begin to investigate the collision, the reconstructionist helps us figure out exactly how it occurred. That helps us determine who is responsible for the collision, and in turn, decide how to pursue the case.

The reconstructionist doesn't stop there. When a case goes to trial, the accident reconstructionist makes it possible for us to explain to the judge and jury exactly what happened, in detail: things like how fast the truck was going, where the truck applied its brakes, how far the truck skidded, how the trailer jackknifed, and where the collision occurred. We'll have the same type of detail regarding our client: where the client was at the time, how fast the client was going, and was stopped or taking other measures to avoid a dangerous situation.

Let me give you an example. I'm getting ready to file a lawsuit right now in this case. Here's what happened: A tractor trailer was coming down a steep grade around 10:30 at night. It was raining hard. The trailer jackknifed and struck our client's car which was going in the same direction.

Our client was killed when the tractor trailer overtook the car and the trailer swung across the lane of travel on the interstate.

The tractor trailer was heading north. The trailer swung across the northbound lane, hit our client from behind, and killed her. We couldn't figure out how it was that the truck was going so much faster. The truck and the client were driving in the same direction. How could the truck have been going so much faster than our client that it lost control and the trailer swung around and hit our client from behind? It basically sheared off the top of her car. How could that have happened?

The deputies and the state trooper who arrived at the scene didn't know. They couldn't figure out what had happened. After we downloaded the computer information from our client's car, we were able to determine that our client had actually been stopped at the time of the collision. Her foot was not on the gas and the car was not moving.

The accident reconstructionist takes that piece of information and says, "Okay, what was going on here? How could she be stopped on the interstate and not moving?" We speculated that because it was raining so hard she had actually pulled off of the interstate and was on the side of the road. So we went back to the client's car, or what was left of it—it was nothing but rubble. We applied power to the car via an external battery and something amazing happened. Her flashers were on. Her hazard lights were on. That's the only thing that would power up. It was no coincidence that the physical evidence (debris from the client's car and a large oil stain) was on the right berm of the road against the guard rail.

This is what the reconstructionist has concluded: Because it was raining so hard, our client had pulled off the side of the road with her flashers on, her hazard lights on and was waiting for the rain to slow down or to stop. Meanwhile the truck was driving at 76 miles an hour down a hill. When it reached the slight turn at the bottom of the hill, the driver lost control, and the reason he overtook our client's car so quickly was that she was parked on the right side berm of the road with her hazard lights on. He never saw her. He never did see her.

These reconstructionists are the experts that we use in these cases to try to figure out what happened. In building a case, we also utilize a whole other category of experts. These we would call damage experts.

Our damage experts come from a variety of fields, from rehabilitation to economics to vocational planning. Survivors of a trucking collision can be left with injuries that will change their lives forever. The case that we build for them needs to take into account all of those changes, and that's where these damage experts are essential.

For instance, just yesterday I was working on another case with an expert in physical rehabilitation. The client in this case—let's call him Charley—has been paralyzed after being hit by a tractor trailer.

Charley's story

Charley's story is particularly tragic. He was coming home from work, just sitting at a stop light, waiting for the light to turn green. The driver of the tractor trailer was distracted and didn't realize the light had turned red. He slammed on his brakes, but couldn't get stopped in time and rear-ended Charley's car. The question is why? Was the driver simply not paying attention? Was he distracted by something? We see that a lot. Was he on his phone? Was he fooling around with his GPS trying to get directions? Was he text messaging? Was he using some other mobile device? Was he tired? Had he driven too many hours?

What we do know is that there was absolutely no excuse for this trucker not to realize that the traffic had stopped. There's probably three-quarters of a mile distance that he could have seen the traffic light and the other cars stopped at the light. The weather was nice. It was a perfectly sunny day; the pavement was dry. Was it just simply a mistake? An accident? Maybe. What we do know is that the truck driver was clearly distracted. There simply no other reasonable explanation for why he did not stop. The driver's carelessness has changed Charley's life forever. He's now paralyzed from the mid-chest down to his toes.

Charley is 57 years old. He has no feeling or sensation from his belly button to the tips of his toes. He is confined to a wheelchair, and he can no longer work.

The rehabilitation expert is putting together a life care plan for Charley. The fact is that when you go to trial, you only have one opportunity to recover. We have to be able to tell the jury what kind of medical care and life care expenses this poor man is going to need for the rest of his life because of the negligence of the trucking company and their driver. We have to plan out things like hospital beds, wheelchairs, attendant care, physical therapy, occupational therapy—all these things that Charley is going to need for the rest of his life. He's 57 years old. He has a life expectancy of late 70s or early 80s. That means we have to project out his life care expenses for 25 to 30 years.

In Charley's case, we have experts in rehabilitation and life care planning. We also have a vocational expert who will evaluate him, because it's doubtful that he will ever be able to return to gainful employment. Once we have the input from all of these experts, we then have an economist who will then calculate the numbers on all of it—lost wages, future medical expenses and future life care expenses—to make a projection of damages. While liability is important, and accident reconstruction is important, it's essential that we be able to accurately project the damages that Charley is going to have or that any client is going to have, because you only get one opportunity to recover those damages for the rest of your life. You can't go to trial, get a verdict, and then come back five years later to say you need more money. That's why all of our experts are so vital to these cases.

We had a similar situation in the case of Donna Collins, the

47-year-old woman whose case I described in the introduction to this book. She was left with severe brain damage, so we brought in a life care planner to look at her living arrangements. Prior to her brain injury, Donna Collins was an independent person. She could walk up and down stairs, get dressed, take care of her own personal hygiene, take a bath, take a shower, drive herself, do all of the normal activities of daily life. Now because of her brain injury she's not able to do any of that. She was living in a two-story house. Now she can't walk up and down the stairs.

What are we going to do about the house and renovations to a house? Donna's bathroom now has to be wheelchair accessible. The shower or the bathtub has to be wheelchair accessible. The sink, the toilet and all of those types of things have to be able to take care of a person who is handicapped. Prior to the collision, she was living in a regular two-story house. It certainly wasn't designed for people who were disabled. Now she's severely disabled. Her family is having to build a home for her—they're in the process right now—so that it's a one-story home with extra-wide doors, with no stairs, with a zero entry shower, with shower chairs and a lift, an automatic lift that will help the family move her and make transfers a whole lot easier instead of having to pick her up all the time.

The life care planning expert was an essential part of our team in that case, looking not only at the medical care needs but also at the living situation to see what modifications need to be made to the home. In cases with severe disabling injuries that's a major part of the damage picture.

Our goal is to make sure that we provide for the client the rest of his or her life. In a situation where a family has lost a loved one, we look for all the benefits that surviving family might be able to recover. What would be the lost wages for the decedent? What would be the decedent's benefits from health insurance, or Medicare, or a 401k? Those are all benefits that a wife or children would be able to recover.

Another question is that of lost household services. Most married couples have some way of dividing up the various tasks that contribute to running a household. If one spouse is suddenly and tragically killed, the survivor is now facing all those tasks and responsibilities alone. If the wife lost her husband, now she might need to hire someone to do things that he used to do at home, perhaps maintenance around the house, cutting the grass, shoveling the snow, taking care of the vehicles. A husband whose wife has been killed might need to hire someone for other services like child care, house cleaning or grocery shopping. Compensation for lost household services can also be part of a damage settlement, and our experts can help to calculate all of those.

Leading the team of experts: Your lawyer

Each of the experts I have talked about in this chapter is important. Most important of all is the person who brings all of these experts and their knowledge together on your behalf. Remember what we said earlier: There is just one opportunity to recover for the rest of your life. You have to have a lawyer who understands that. You have to have a lawyer who has the connections and the expert witnesses who are able to accurately project those important damages.

Let's go back to Charley's case. The trucking company says, "We have a million dollars in insurance coverage." Well, that's not going to be enough. His medical bills are already in excess of $125,000, just for what he's already had. That doesn't begin to cover what he's going to need down the road.

As Charley's lawyers, our job also is to find any and all parties who bear some responsibility in his case. We start with the trucking company and their driver, and then we ask, are there other companies that rightfully share in the responsibility for causing this tragedy? There may be what we call joint venture, meaning that there may be more than one company involved in the collision. For instance, we will look at the load the truck was carrying. Was it a brokered load, meaning that there is a third party with liability or responsibility in this case, where insurance might be found? In Charley's case, we have found that there is a joint venture with at least one other company. That company is equally liable for Charley's injuries. The insurance coverage from the second company will help pay for Charley's medical and life-care expenses.

A person trying to do this on their own, or a lawyer who doesn't routinely do this kind of work, is likely to see a million dollars of coverage and think, "Great, that's a lot of money." But in Charley's circumstances that's barely any money. In fact that's virtually no money. He's going to have 20-25 years of being in a wheelchair, and living with all of the medical complications that come along with being a paraplegic. A million dollars, while it sounds like a lot of money, is nothing in these circumstances. So my job is not only to determine what the rules and regulations the truck driver and the company broke, but also to determine what other companies are responsible for this man's injuries, and what other insurance may apply. Our job is to fairly and ethically find as much insurance coverage as we possibly can find from the parties who are rightfully responsible.

Chapter 7

You Need Better Insurance

Most of the concepts we have been discussing in this book deal with the aftermath of a collision. Taking a good look at your insurance coverage is something that you can and should do today, *before* you need to draw on it. I hope you'll never need to draw on it, but if you do, you will be very glad that you have purchased enough insurance.

Why? One of the most difficult parts of my job is explaining to any client who has been seriously injured, or to a family who has lost a loved one, is that there is not enough insurance coverage to compensate them for the claim. Claims in these trucking cases can involve hundreds of thousands of dollars in medical bills. They can involve tens of thousands, or even hundreds of thousands dollars in lost wages. They can involve property damage. They can involve rehabilitation expenses and life care expenses that can go into the millions of dollars.

All of these things are extremely expensive. For example, it costs in excess of $25,000 to be transported by helicopter from the scene of an accident to a local hospital, and I think that's a pretty typical fee throughout the United States. Even though the helicopter transport might be a just 15 minute flight, you can count on the helicopter expenses alone to be in the $25,000 range. That's just one of the many expenses following a major collision. It takes a lot of money to cover these types of damages and these types of claims.

But the average person buying car insurance is usually just

trying to get on the road and licensed as quickly and as cheaply as possible. The insurance coverage that is often purchased is the minimum amount of coverage that the state requires. That's a mistake.

I can't state this more clearly: Minimum coverage is not enough. It is a mistake, and it can be a very costly mistake.

With insurance, as with most things in life, you get what you pay for. And every day, I see what happens when people don't have enough insurance. I listen to clients rant when they're angry because the at-fault driver had only $25,000 of insurance coverage. "How could somebody be driving around with only $25,000? And they damn near killed me!" Chances are, when you look at the client's insurance, you find that it's exactly the same: $25,000 of coverage. If the client had been at fault and seriously injured somebody, they themselves would have only had $25,000 of coverage. It's understandable. Everybody is looking to pay as little as they possibly can to cover themselves legally and be able to drive their vehicle. That's completely understandable. It's still a mistake! The truth is $25,000 of insurance coverage is nothing in today's world. As I said today, the helicopter ride alone will cost you more than $25,000.

You might expect that if you are involved in a collision with a truck, the trucking company's insurance will be enough. You can't assume that. Even trucking companies have limited insurance. Companies make every attempt to keep their insurance premiums to a minimum, just as individuals do.

We work on cases where there might be a million dollars of insurance coverage. I know that sounds like a lot, but after you pay your medical bills back, and after you pay for the litigation, and after you take account of your lost wages, a million dollars ends up not being very much money at all.

What kind of insurance should you have?

When I have the opportunity, I encourage people to buy as much *uninsured motorist coverage* and as much *underinsured motorist coverage* as they can afford, because that kind of insurance coverage will often come into play. For example, what if you are involved in a truck collision and the trucking company doesn't have any insurance? Some of these trucking companies don't. Then you're left with having to chase a bankrupt trucking company, and the litigation will end up costing you far more than you will ever receive. On the other hand, if you have substantial uninsured motorist coverage, then you can collect that from your own insurance carrier.

The same is true with underinsured motorist coverage. Underinsurance comes into play after the insurance coverage of the "at-fault" driver is exhausted. Once that "at-fault" insurance is gone, your underinsurance will kick in and continue to cover your lost wages, medical expenses, rehabilitation expenses, and other such expenses. That coverage is not terribly expensive, but unfortunately I have seen case after case, and client after client, who have only the state minimum coverage. They don't have underinsurance, or if they do, it is the state minimum, and they have state minimum uninsured coverage, all because they just want to get on the road, and they want to be legal. No one ever thinks the accident or the collision is going to happen to them. And then when it does happen to them, it's too late. So we encourage everybody to purchase as much uninsured and underinsured coverage as they can possibly afford.

Affordability is always an issue in purchasing insurance, but remember, uninsured motorist coverage is mandatory. You have no choice but to buy uninsured motorist coverage. The amount of uninsured motorist coverage you can buy is limited by to the amount of liability coverage that you are purchasing. Liability coverage is what applies if you hit someone and you are at fault. It's the coverage that you buy to protect somebody else. If you're going to buy $25,000 of liability coverage, then your insurance company will allow you to purchase a maximum of $25,000 of uninsured motorist coverage. The reason for that maximum is that the law doesn't allow you to protect yourself for an amount more than you are protecting others. That is also true with underinsured motorist coverage.

The difference between the two is that underinsurance is optional coverage. You're not required to buy it, but we strongly recommend that you buy as much underinsured coverage as you can afford. Both uninsured motorist and underinsured motorist coverage are relatively inexpensive.

Neither of these is terribly expensive. At least, do yourself a favor and get a quote. It can make a huge difference if you are involved in a collision with someone who does not have insurance or whose insurance coverage is at a state minimum or is just simply not enough to cover your damages. Underinsured coverage is absolutely invaluable.

We also encourage our clients to purchase what's called *medical payments coverage*. This is coverage that you can buy through your own auto insurance carrier that will pay your medical expenses, no matter who was at fault in the collision. That coverage will range between $500.00 and $25,000.00, depending on how much the client purchases. The average is $5,000.00. In a lot of these trucking cases, that can make a critical difference because it pays the medical bills, or helps pay the medical bills, while the case is in litigation. These cases can take a long time to be resolved. Healthcare providers, doctors, and hospitals are not willing to wait a year, a year and a half, or two years for the case to get resolved before they get paid. The medical payments coverage option will help the client who has been injured by helping the client pay those medical bills while the litigation is ongoing.

One of the most common misunderstandings in this business—I hear it from clients all the time—is the assumption that the "at fault" driver's insurance company is going to pay the medical bills *as they are incurred* by the person who has been injured. In other words if you have to go to the hospital, then that driver's insurance company will pay your hospital bill, and if you have to go to physical therapy, then they'll pay your physical therapy bill or your doctor's bills. That is *not* how it works. The "at-fault" driver's insurance coverage will pay the medical expenses at the end of the case. They will pay only one time. That one time will include those medical bills, lost wages, attorney fees, litigation expenses and life care expenses. But they pay only one time, at the end of the case, and that could be a year, or even longer, after the case has been started.

People need to understand that there has to be a way to pay those medical bills on an ongoing basis while the case is in litigation. That first line of payment is your medical payments coverage. That's why it is so important. You can buy that through your own insurance carrier. The second line of payment for your medical bills will be your health insurance. It will be your Blue Cross Blue Shield, your Aetna, maybe Medicare or Medicaid. It could be Obamacare. Whatever your health insurance coverage is, that will come in second, after your medical payments coverage.

After both the medical payment coverage (if purchased by the client) and the health insurance have been utilized, if there are any copays or other items that are not covered by health insurance, then we do what is called a *letter of protection*. A letter of protection is a letter from the law firm to the healthcare provider that says, "Look. Jane Doe has been involved in a serious collision. Litigation is pending over that collision. Please do not send Ms. Doe to collections. Please do not try to collect the medical bill from her directly. Jane Doe will pay you—out of the settlement of the case." The letter is basically a way of holding off the healthcare provider by promising them that they will get payment out of the settlement. That's called a letter of protection. Not all healthcare providers will accept a letter of protection and if they do not the client will have to figure out a payment plan between themselves and the healthcare provider to keep the outstanding bills from being sent to a collection agency.

There is one other insurance coverage that I encourage every client to consider, and that is a *personal umbrella policy*. A personal umbrella policy will provide the client and their family with coverage up to about as much as you want, with typical umbrella policies covering anywhere from $2-5 million in coverage. Again, they are not terribly expensive. Seek out the advice of a local insurance representative in your community about a personal umbrella policy that will protect you if you are at fault in a collision. You will be protected up to the amount of the umbrella policy and will be provided with the additional coverage you need if you are hit by somebody who does not have coverage or does not have enough coverage.

It's probably a bit more expensive but if you are involved in a serious collision where someone has been killed, or someone has been seriously injured, a personal umbrella policy can really make the difference. It can change someone's life by providing them an appropriate level of insurance coverage.

These are my recommendations: uninsured coverage, underinsured coverage, and an umbrella policy. Those are the three different coverages, along with medical payments coverage, that are vitally important to people. I encourage everyone to speak to their insurance agent about each of those four options.

One more expert: Your insurance representative

I've offered my recommendations on the coverage you should have, but the best recommendation I can make on insurance is that you speak to a local insurance representative. In today's world everyone wants to buy insurance online or over the phone. Everyone is looking for the cheapest insurance possible just to make sure they are legal, and just so that they have an insurance certificate to show the state trooper if they get pulled over.

I strongly recommend that clients engage the services of a local insurance representative in their own community. Sit down and talk with them about your insurance needs. It is very difficult to buy the appropriate coverage online when you have no one to address your questions. It can be hard to get a straight answer from a representative in an online chat or even over the phone.

I urge all of my clients—and I encourage my readers—to engage the services of a local insurance agent, whether it's your local Nationwide agent, State Farm agent, Allstate agent, or whoever it might be. Go down and sit with your local agent, tell them your circumstances, let them know what you can afford, listen to their advice, and buy your insurance coverage that way. You will be much better served that way.

I can't overstate the importance of making sure you have enough insurance. We see it every day. In our office right now, we have four or five cases that would be multimillion dollar cases if there were sufficient insurance coverage, but in each of them there is $100,000 of insurance coverage or less. Because the insurance coverage is so minimal, these cases that would otherwise be worth maybe three million dollars are now worth $50,000. And in cases like these, the injured parties simply cannot be made whole.

Yes, you can pursue the at-fault driver for an amount above their coverage limit but those people don't have $400,000, $500,000, or a million dollars of assets just lying around. They don't have that kind of cash, and they don't have property that doesn't already have a lien on it, so most often, the value of these cases is determined by the amount of insurance coverage that's available. It seems unfair but it's the reality of the situation

We just settled a case in which the client had more than $400,000 in medical bills. The at-fault driver had $100,000 of coverage. We end up settling the case for $100,000. It would have cost too much money to pursue the at-fault driver who ultimately doesn't have any money or any other assets to recover. It doesn't make sense to spend $50,000 of that $100,000 settlement to go after someone who doesn't have any money to pay you. So what might well have been a two-and-a-half to three million dollar case is now only worth $100,000 because there wasn't enough insurance coverage.

This is the best advice I can give on this subject: You can't force the general public to buy more coverage, but you have the opportunity to protect yourself against those who do not buy enough insurance coverage. Take the opportunity now while you're healthy, you're well, you have a job, and things are going well for you. Take the opportunity now to buy as much insurance coverage as you can afford to protect yourself and your family.

Chapter 8

Trucking Companies Never Disclose Details

If you have the misfortune to be involved in a collision with a truck, do not make the mistake of expecting the trucking company to be open and forthcoming with you. That will not happen. No trucking company is ever going to admit to the injured victim or to the family members of someone who has been killed in a truck collision that their truck driver fell asleep at the wheel because he had been driving too many hours. The company is never going to disclose that the truck's brakes were bad and that's why the truck couldn't be stopped. They are never going to admit that the truck was overloaded, or that the load was improperly secured and that's why the truck driver lost control. They are never going to admit those details to the person who has been injured or to the family of someone who has been killed. In fact I have seen trucking companies that have written policies prohibiting the truck driver from admitting fault.

The reason that the trucking company is so reluctant to disclose these details is simple: They know that liability often drives the ultimate value of a case. The case is not just about the costs of medical expenses, lost wages, rehab expenses, or a victim's lasting scars. All of those things are always part of the case—sometimes a large part—but the final value of a case is often driven by the degree of bad conduct by the trucking company.

Let me give you an example. Suppose we have a case in which there's $100,000 of medical bills and there is $25,000 of lost wages. In addition there will obviously be some compensation for pain and suffering, so the case might be valued at, say, $350,000.

What if we discover that this is the second or third time that this truck driver has been in a rear-end accident because he's been texting on his phone while driving the vehicle? Or we find out that this is the sixth or seventh time that the trucking company has been cited by the National Transportation Administration for allowing their truck drivers to drive more than the allotted amount of time? With that added information, the same case might now be worth three, four, five, maybe six million dollars.

We have to realize that while damages in a case are always important, the value of the case may eventually lie with how significant the liability claim is against the trucking company. If the trucking company has lied, if the trucking company has covered up, if the trucking company has committed a fraud— and we see these things on a regular basis—that is going to upset a jury. And when a jury gets angry about the conduct of a trucking company, especially repeatedly bad conduct, or lying, or fraud, that anger will drive up the value of the case significantly. A case originally valued at $350,000 could be worth multiple millions of dollars, if they allow the lawyer to conduct discovery and start figuring out why the tractor trailer rear-ended the person at the intersection. It could be a simple mistake. Maybe the driver looked at the radio and all of a sudden he didn't realize how close he was, and he couldn't avoid the collision. But maybe the collision happened because he was texting and driving, or maybe it happened because he fell asleep since he had been driving 22 straight hours. Maybe it happened because the brakes were worn out, and the trucking company knew, or should have known, that the brakes were worn out, and this has happened to them before. The facts and the circumstances surrounding the accident, and whether it could have been avoided, will significantly affect the value of the case.

The trucking companies and their insurance companies

know very well that their liability directly affects the value of a case. They also know something else. They know that the injured victim is going to need money. Their medical bills are piling up. They can't go to work because they're injured. They hurt. They are confused. They're afraid. They're anxious. They're unsure of what to do next because this is a brand new situation for them. They've never had to deal with something like this before, and it is overwhelming. The insurance companies for the trucking companies, and the trucking companies themselves know, that the faster they can get to the injured victim or their family the better off the trucking company will be in the long run. Not the better off the victim will be, but the better off the trucking company will be. Why? Because if they can put $100,000 in somebody's pocket today, that client is going to think, "Wow, that's a lot of money," and that trucking company can easily save itself millions of dollars. They know that it will cost them much more if a lawyer gets involved for the victim, and they want to avoid that at all costs.

The trucking company, or their insurance company, is going to be very nice to the person who has been injured or to the family of someone who has been killed. They will act as though they are looking out for the victim's best interests. They will be pleasant and they will be concerned and they will seem sympathetic, but at the end of the day, the insurance company or the trucking company has only one interest, and that's protecting the assets and money of the insurance company and the trucking company. They are not interested in protecting the rights of the injured person. That's why people need a lawyer.

That's why people need us, so that we can step up and say, "Look. We are here. We are standing here on behalf of the injured victim. We are standing up on behalf of the family whose husband, wife, father, or child was killed by a truck. We will stand for them because we represent them and we protect their interests."

The insurance company and the trucking company are there to protect the interests of the insurance company and the trucking company. Make no mistake about it. They are there to protect their company's interests, and they are smart about it. They know that when money is tight, when people aren't able to work, when medical bills are rolling in, when the victim is most vulnerable, that's the time to strike and try to get a quick settlement. The quicker they can settle, the cheaper it is for the trucking company. Don't let that happen to you. Call a lawyer. We want you to call us but most importantly call a lawyer. Let the lawyer evaluate the case, let them direct you, and let them give you advice. This is what we do every day. We protect victims of truck accidents. That is our job and we are good at it!

One of the things that you need to understand is the statute of limitations on these cases. Here in West Virginia and Ohio, for example, the statute of limitations is two years. That means that people have two years to bring a case. There's no hurry. There is certainly an urgency for us to investigate, to take witness statements, and to reconstruct the accident. We want to do that immediately. But the truth of the matter is that people should not want to settle the case early on because they don't yet know what additional medical needs might arise down the road. Are they going to need another surgery? Are they going to need physical therapy? Are they going to need a wheelchair? What are they going to need?

Remember, once you settle the case—once you sign the release and take the money—the case is over forever. I tell people the release means three things. It means 1) the case is over, 2) the case is over, and 3) the case is over! If six months later you suddenly need physical therapy, or you are going to need another surgery and you hadn't really anticipated it, that's too bad. You can't go back and get more money from the trucking company or their insurance carrier. You took the money, you signed the release, and the case is over. There's no coming back.

We do not settle a case until the client is finished treating. I want to be certain before I recommend a settlement value to a client, or recommend a settlement to a client, that we are reasonably confident that there's not going to be any additional treatment. Of course there's no way to guarantee the future, but we want to be reasonably certain that physical therapy, or another surgery, or additional rehabilitation will not be necessary. We want to know that they have recovered or have reached their maximum improvement. On cases where the client needs significant treatment into the future or perhaps for the rest of their lives, we use experts in the field of life care planning to project out these costs which are then part of the settlement equation. Because once you settle the case, the case is over.

Don't be taken in by scare tactics

Insurance companies know that people are scared. They just got the ambulance bill, and they just got the hospital bill, and the expenses are piling up. The normal human reaction is, "Oh my gosh, what are we going to do now? I can't get back to work." And here comes the insurance company. They're knocking on the door and saying, "Look, here's $50,000, you're going to need this money. You ought to take this money. You don't need those lawyers. All they do is take your money. Take the fifty grand and let's be done with this." The problem is, people get scared. They're anxious and they don't know where to turn, so they take the money, and then it's over. The insurance company and the trucking company walk away, and they are done, and there's not a darn thing more that they can do about it.

Don't let them scare you away from going to an attorney. Remember the title of this chapter: Trucking companies never disclose details. Left to their own devices, the trucking companies are never going to tell you what they did wrong. Their position will be, "Oh, it was an accident. Sorry about that." They will apologize and they will be nice to you, but they are never going to tell you the details about why the accident happened. They are never going to tell you that it happened six months earlier, and that it happened again eight months before that. Remember that the trucking companies are in business to make money. That's their sole motivation. That's what motivates them to take more loads. That's what motivates them to make more runs. That's what motivates them to keep those trucks on the road. That's what motivates them to keep the driver behind the wheel. Keeping the driver behind the wheel means they can take more loads, and taking more loads means making more money.

If the trucking company is playing by the rules, and having their drivers stop, and pull over, and sleep the required amount of time, that's less money that they're making. If they are pulling that truck off the road to fix its brakes on a regular basis, or to change the tires, that costs the trucking company money in materials, parts, equipment, and labor to repair the truck, and it also costs the company money to keep the truck off the road. The company's financial incentive is always to do more with less—to go further with less sleep, to drive longer with faulty brakes, to put as much of a load in that truck as it can possibly haul—because they make more money that way. It's more dangerous, but they will run that risk. Why? Because in every collision between a truck and a car, the truck always wins. One hundred percent of the time, the truck wins.

All of this means that the trucking company has a financial incentive not to play by the rules. That can also apply to its investigation of any collision. Most, if not all, trucking companies do have policies and procedures within their company requiring an internal investigation into these accidents.

For example, when a tractor trailer is involved in a truck collision, often times the company's own policies and procedures will require an accident committee to investigate the cause of the accident was, who was at fault, how it could have been avoided, and how it could be prevented.

The problem is that these investigations are often inaccurate and intentionally incomplete. These trucking companies will not conscientiously investigate a collision involving one of their own trucks, especially if the truck or the truck driver was at fault. We have had numerous cases where we have gotten the trucking company's incident report or internal investigation report of the collision at hand, and it has been completely false.

I know that seems incredible, but I have seen these reports that are completely false and fraudulent. They simply make up things that did not occur, or they omit huge parts of the facts from their investigation, so their report does not portray the trucking company or the driver to be at fault even when they clearly were.

We are working on a case like that right now. If you read the investigation report from the trucking company, and you compared it to the actual facts from the case and to the police report, you would think they were talking about two different collisions.

A trucking company will never ever voluntarily accept the blame. They will never voluntarily say, "Our driver was fatigued and should not have been driving." They will never voluntarily say that the brakes were worn out. They will never say that on their own and they will never put that in the investigation report.

What they *will* do is blame the other driver. They will blame the victim, especially if that victim has been killed, because that victim cannot speak for himself or herself. They will blame weather conditions. They will blame everything under the sun, but they will never take responsibility themselves.

The trucking company will never point a finger at itself and say, "This was our mistake. This was our fault." They will certainly blame the victim for sure. They will blame unknown drivers who pulled out in front of them. They will blame everything they possibly can, but they will never accept responsibility for their own wrongdoing.

I've been doing this a long time, and I have never seen it happen where a trucking company has accepted full responsibility for its own wrongdoing.

We simply cannot rely solely on the trucking company's own investigation. We do our own investigation, and we also use the official accident report.

The accident report is a publicly available document from the investigating agency. It could be state troopers, deputy sheriffs, or city police, depending on who did the original investigation at the scene. All you have to do is pay the fee, send in a request, and you will get the police report. Those reports are generally accurate. They are produced by the law enforcement officers who are taking statements immediately after the accident.

These law enforcement professionals are the first ones on scene. They are the first responders who are taking photographs, making measurements, taking statements, and finding out what happened. They are generally accurate, though there exceptions, especially when the law enforcement officials are stretched too thin.

When these first responders get done with this accident, they're often called to another one. Then after that one, it's another one 20 miles further down the interstate. They don't have the time or the resources to devote to a meticulous reconstruction of a trucking collision.

They don't have the time to do it and they don't have the money to do it. In a complex case, they may not have the expertise. They are good people trying to do the very best they can, but their responsibilities vary. Maybe right now they're investigating a truck collision, but an hour and a half from now, they're going to be chasing down somebody who robbed a convenience store.

No one can be an expert in everything. While these official accident reports are generally reliable, it is important to do a meticulous accident reconstruction by someone who does have the expertise, and the time, and the resources to do that.

Here's an example from a case we finished not long ago.

The company in this case was a utility company. Their driver was driving a large Ford F350 pickup truck—a big, heavy-duty truck—carrying all of the equipment that one would need to do the job. The driver was texting and driving at the same time, and he was in a horrific collision where he rear-ended our clients, who were driving *in the same direction* on the same four-lane highway.

The clients were a married couple. The collision killed the husband and injured the wife. It was a straight stretch of road. If the driver had been paying attention, he could have seen our clients for at least half a mile, or three-quarters of a mile, maybe even further.

In our own investigation, we did an actual drive-through. We had a video camera mounted on the dash of the car so that we could see the line of sight that would have be available to this truck driver. It was at least three-quarters of a mile.

The utility company's report of their internal investigation made it sound as though the truck driver crested the top of a hill, and that our clients were driving so slowly that when he crested the top of the hill, there was no way for him to avoid running into the back of their car.

I presented the truck driver with the report from the utility company that employed hm. When I read it to him, and I showed it to him, and he had it in his hand, I said, "Mr. Smith, is this accurate?" He looked at me and said, "No, it is not." I said, "In fact, it is completely false isn't it?" He said, "You are correct. This is false."

I said, "Mr. Smith, you had nearly a mile to have recognized my clients, who were in the right lane, on a straight stretch of road and were traveling slower than you were, and you had plenty of time to avoid this collision if you had been paying attention." He said, "Mr. Colombo, that is true."

If you had read the report prepared by the utility, it appeared that the truck driver crested the hill, my two clients—who were senior citizens—were simply driving too slow, and this truck driver just did not have enough time to react. That was an outright lie, and the truck driver admitted to it.

I wish I could tell you that this is a unique story, but it is not.

Remember Charley's story, which we discussed in Chapter Six? The circumstances of his accident were similar. He was stopped at a traffic light, along with several other vehicles, and he was rear-ended by a tractor trailer. Now he is a paraplegic.

The truck driver who hit Charley had probably half a mile or more to see that traffic light and to see that the traffic was stopped. In fact, about a quarter of mile before that intersection, there were flashing lights on either side of the road. You've seen this sort of thing—flashing lights to warn oncoming traffic that they are approaching an intersection with a red light. The truck driver simply plowed into the back of Charley's car, ricocheted off him and then hit three other people at this intersection.

Charley is paralyzed from the waist down. In the statement given by the truck driver, he indicates that the traffic suddenly stopped in front of him, that he could not stop in time, and that's why he ran into the back of all of these cars. What he said was that the four other cars that were involved stopped suddenly because of an accident in front of them and that's why he couldn't get stopped in time and he ran into Charley.

That was a complete lie. There *was* no other accident. These cars were stopped for a considerable period of time waiting on the red light to turn green. There was no other accident; there was no sudden stop. This driver simply wasn't paying attention.

But he wouldn't just admit that and say, "Look, I'm sorry, I wasn't paying attention. I made a mistake." And frankly, that happens to everybody. We all have been distracted by the radio station, or talking to somebody, or eating French fries, or whatever it might be. But instead of saying, "I made a mistake; I wasn't paying attention," he tried to blame it on the cars in front of him suddenly stopping. These cars had been stopped for minutes. By the way, this is one of those trucking companies that has a written policy instructing its drivers to never admit fault.

Trucking companies will say and do anything to avoid taking responsibility for unlawful conduct or wrongdoing. What they love to do most is blame the victim. They love to blame the victim, especially if the victim is deceased, has been killed, or has been injured to the point where they can't testify for themselves. Then it becomes the company's word against no one's. Always remember that the favorite defense of a trucking company is to blame the victim. Don't let that happen to you.

Chapter 9

You Must Repay Your Medical Bills

This is an important topic because I find that it confuses many clients. When you are involved in a claim or suit following a collision, at some point you will hear the word *subrogation*, which is a legal term. Webster's defines subrogation as "the assumption by a third party (as a second creditor or an insurance company) of another's legal right to collect a debt or damages." Never mind the legalese; here's what this means for you.

You will remember that in Chapter Seven, we talked about insurance coverage and who pays medical bills, as they are incurred, prior to a settlement in the case. What you need to understand is that when your medical bills are paid by health insurance, whether it's Medicare, Medicaid, Blue Cross Blue Shield, or any other health insurance, you need to pay the insurer back for those medical bills. That is subrogation.

At the end of the case, if the injured person gets a settlement from the trucking company or their insurance carrier, any type of health insurance must be reimbursed for the medical expenses that they have paid. If the health insurance carrier has paid $100,000 of medical bills, and you get a settlement in the case, your health insurance is going to expect to be paid back from the settlement for the medical bills that they have paid. This is a universal issue; it applies in every state. This is particularly important in Medicare and Medicaid cases, because the government will actively seek repayment. If you settle your case for $300,000 and you owe Medicare $100,000, believe me that

Medicare will be coming after their $100,000. And if you have already spent your $300,000, they're still coming after you.

So we call that subrogation, and subrogation comes out of a settlement of the case. It's important, and people often forget about it. If they settle the case they think, "Well, my health insurance carrier paid the medical bills. This money's mine." No, it's not. You will have to repay your health insurance carrier out of the settlement proceeds. The subrogation amount—the amount you have to pay back to the insurance carrier—comes out of the settlement along with your attorney's fees and litigation expenses. You as the client receive the net after those amounts are subtracted. That's the way it is in every case, with every lawyer, and in every state.

It's important to be aware of this, especially if you decide to try to settle a case yourself. The danger for someone trying to settle a case on their own is that they don't understand the ins and outs of subrogation. As a lawyer in these cases, often the biggest part of my job is to negotiate the subrogation amounts. We are there to negotiate not only with the insurance company of the at-fault driver, but also with Medicare, and Medicaid, and the health insurance companies, so that we can get the most favorable result for our client.

At the end of the day, it's about how much money the client ultimately receives. After the medical expenses are paid, after lost wages are reimbursed, after the lawyers are paid, after all of that, what does the client get to put in his or her pocket? A large part of what we do is negotiating the *subrogation lien*. (A *lien* is the fancy legal term for an amount owed.) These negotiations can be complicated and time-consuming, and they are a huge part of what we do here at Colombo Law. The subrogation liens—and the way they are resolved—can make all the difference between clients being pleased with the result of their case and clients being very disappointed with their result.

I'm always surprised how many people don't realize that

paying back the health insurance carrier comes out of their settlement. That's not unique to our cases. It's done that way in every case, with every law firm, in every state.

The logic behind this is that if you're insurance carrier has already paid for the medical bills, and you receive settlement money that includes these bills then you would essentially be getting paid twice for the same expense.

The health insurance company's position is that they fronted the bills and paid for them. You use those same bills as part of your claim, and once you are paid by the at-fault driver's insurance company for those bills, they should be reimbursed. This may sound a little complicated, but it's actually pretty simple, and there's a good reason for doing it this way. The reason that you want health insurance to pay the medical bills is that they usually have already negotiated payment rates with most healthcare providers. Blue Cross/Blue Shield, for example, is certainly not paying the hospital bill at a hundred cents on the dollar. So in subrogation, we only have to pay Blue Cross back for what they actually paid, not what was billed.

Suppose you were injured in WV and brought a claim. Suppose further that the hospital bill is $100,000, but Blue Cross/Blue Shield, based on their rate with the hospital, only has to pay $50,000. In this case, we make a claim for the original $100,000 medical bill, but we only have to pay $50,000 back to Blue Cross/Blue Shield. In addition, when you have a lawyer, the attorney fee is usually deducted from what you have to pay them as well. For instance, if there is a 40 percent attorney fee, the health insurance will usually deduct 40 percent of what you have to pay them. Basically, the client has hired us to be the bill collector, and so the health insurer pays their pro rata share of the attorney bill. That comes in the form of a reduction in the lien. So in this circumstance, the client would have to pay back only $30,000.00 of the lien. Remember, there could still be co-pays and other out of pocket portions of the bill that still need to be paid by the client but the point is there is a significant benefit.

Other states have different rules on how much of the medical bill can be presented to the jury. Is it the amount billed or is it the amount payed? Often times there is a big difference between the amounts billed verses the amount paid. For example, Ohio allows the trucking company to put both numbers into evidence-the amount billed and the amount paid. This is a benefit to the trucking company because the thinking is that the jury would likely only award the client the amount of medical bills that were actually paid not the amount billed. These are issues that need to be addressed by a lawyer who knows the ins and outs of what can be a complicated situation.

Please understand that the health insurance company is responsible for paying the medical bills regardless of who is at fault. And because the victim hired an attorney to pursue the trucking company, and has paid an attorney to do that, they are in essence doing the health insurance company's work for them. So the health insurance company generally ends up reducing the amount of the lien by the percentage of the attorney's fees. The one exception to that is what we call ERISA plans, which are employee-sponsored plans. Depending on the language of an ERISA plan, that can get very complicated, and the attorney's fees may not be able to be deducted.

Although our team negotiates subrogation, it doesn't change what we receive in fees. It *does* benefit the client, and client satisfaction is first and foremost with us.

What can you expect in a settlement?

This is the question everyone asks: what can I expect to receive from a settlement in my case? As you might expert it varies widely. The facts of the case, the seriousness of the damages, the jurisdiction that the case is being brought and the amount of insurance coverage available are just a few of the many factors that influence the value of the case. What I tell my clients is that after all is said and done—after the attorneys are paid, after the litigation expenses are paid, after medical expenses and subrogation has been satisfied—the client can generally expect to receive about 50 to 55 percent of the settlement amount.

There are a number of different expenses involved, but everything comes out of a settlement.

As attorneys, we handle cases on what's called a *contingency fee* basis. That means that clients do not pay us up front. Clients do not write a check every time they meet with me or whenever we do work on their case. We get paid a percentage of what is recovered when the case is settled in favor of the client or when we go to trial and there's a verdict in favor of the client. This is typically a no-risk situation for the client. If there is no recovery, there are no attorney's fees.

Our fee percentages will vary a bit depending on the circumstances of the case—sometimes higher, sometimes lower. The important point is that if we do not settle a case in favor of the client, then there are *no* attorney's fees. Zero.

There are litigation expenses, such as filing fees and deposition fees and expert fees, that apply because the state bar in most states requires that the clients be responsible for those expenses, but our law firm advances those expenses. We get reimbursed for them out of the settlement.

After attorney's fees and litigation expenses are deducted, and after medical expenses and subrogation is paid, meaning that the health insurance carrier has been reimbursed, the client can expect to receive, on average, between 50 and 55 percent of the total recovery. It does vary. Sometimes it's a little more; sometimes it's a little less.

What I want to emphasize is that this is a no-risk situation for the client. There are no attorney's fees if there's no recovery. We receive a percentage of the recovery, and if for whatever reason we are not successful, the client owes no attorney's fees.

We want the client to be happy with us. Just today, as I'm writing this, we waived our entire fee on a case. There wasn't enough insurance and we knew that if we waived our fee, that would give us credibility with the health insurance company to get them to waive their lien, so that's what we did. We were able to persuade the health insurance company to waive their lien, and because of that we were able to put $120,000 in our client's pocket today. It was the right thing to do. Because of his accident, this poor fellow had lost his leg; it was amputated below the knee. He had almost $400,000 in bills and between the lien and my fee, he would have been left with nothing. We could not allow that to happen. That's not what we're about. This client is a younger gentleman, a very nice man with a wonderful family. We could not allow him to lose his leg because of someone's negligence, and then for us to get paid and health insurance to get paid and him to be left with nothing. That could not happen. So we waived our fee. That allowed us to go to the health insurance company to argue with them to say "Look, this poor guy needs help, and we want to help him. We are willing to waive our fee, and we are going to ask that you do the same." And they did. So what looked like zero recovery for him went to $120,000, which was the maximum amount of insurance coverage available. I just gave him the check an hour ago. Those are the things you have to do. That's the way this works, the way we do it.

This is a business for us, and of course, we are here to make money. But our business will be short-lived if our clients are not happy with the services that we provide. There are cases on which we could make money, but as a friend of mine once told me, "Just because you can, doesn't mean you should."

He told me that 25 years ago, and it has stayed with me ever since. "Just because you can, doesn't mean you should." We had a fee agreement in this case, and I'm sure the clients would have understood. They would have paid our fee. We spent the time, we did a good job negotiating the case, and we could have taken a fee. But the truth is you shouldn't take a fee in those circumstances. We've done that many times. Why? Because I still have both legs, and I'm still able to walk, and my family will get by just fine. That family needed the help. So you do the right thing.

Conclusion

I hope that the information I have shared in this book will help you, or your family, should you find yourself involved in a trucking collision.

In the Introduction, I described these collisions as an epidemic in our country. Are there remedies for this epidemic? I wouldn't say there is a remedy, or a complete solution, but there are things that we can do.

Drive defensively

The first and best thing that you personally can do to protect yourself is defensive driving. You need to be extraordinarily alert and careful of driving around all vehicles, especially trucks. Whenever there is a truck versus car collision, the truck always wins. It's no contest.

I look at this as taking personal responsibility. The best advice I could give you on this topic is—put your phone away, slow down and wear your seatbelt. By driving defensively and paying attention you will reduce your risk of being in a collision substantially. Also, keep in mind that the drivers of these trucks find themselves in blind spots. The road can be especially narrow for these large trucks with not much room to maneuver. These drivers have been on the road for a long time and may be fatigued. They may be using equipment that is worn out or doesn't work properly. As we've seen in this book, these truckers are sometimes forced into situations that they would probably prefer not to be in. Traffic may be heavy, or it may be moving very fast. There may be construction zones that the driver didn't anticipate or expect.

Protect yourself, slow down and pay attention. When things go bad with a truck, they go bad fast and without warning.

Addressing the national epidemic

The one thing that could diminish this epidemic would be for the trucking companies to slow down. What I mean by slow down is not just the speed of the trucks on the road but slow down *generally*. Slow down and make sure the driver is qualified, slow down and make sure the driver is not fatigued, slow down and make sure the truck is properly maintained, etc. Unfortunately, the companies have no incentive to do that. Their entire business model is built around more loads, more trucks, more miles, and more speed. If any company were to slow down voluntarily, it would lose any competitive advantage and would quickly be run out of business.

Is there a national solution to this problem? More legislation doesn't seem to be an answer. There is a lot of legislation out there already. As we've seen, there are plenty of rules and regulations aimed at keeping people safe. And many of these collisions are not accidents; they are preventable violations of these rules. But as long as the financial incentives outweigh the risk of skirting the regulations, companies will continue to do whatever they can to get around the rules.

The only real way to eliminate this epidemic is to take away the economic incentives that push trucking companies and drivers to put profits above safety. I don't expect to see that happen any time soon; it's not realistic. These companies push drivers harder and further, and push the trucks themselves harder and further, because they are incentivized to do so. They make more money by hauling more loads and by hauling heavier loads. They make more money by going further and farther with trucks that are worn out, with brakes and tires that are worn out, with drivers who are too tired, with trucks that are overloaded, and with loads that are not properly secured.

We can't legislate our way out of this situation. Realistically, the money is too significant to get these guys to slow down, to use better equipment, and to meet all of the regulations. We have enough regulations. If these trucking companies would follow the regulations that are already in place, these trucks would be safer, the drivers would be safer, and the general driving public would be safer.

Enforcement of the existing regulations could be better. According to the FMCSA's *Pocket Guide to Large Truck and Bus Statistics 2016*, the number of roadside inspections has been decreasing since 2011. So has the number of traffic violation inspections. There are more and more trucks on the road, but less enforcement activity.

There are simply not enough enforcement resources available. The trucking companies and their drivers know that. They know how to get past the weigh stations and the inspections. We have had drivers tell us, "We know when the inspectors are going to be out. We know what routes to take to avoid the random stops." These guys are smart, especially if they're driving the same route on a regular basis. They know when the enforcement is out there. Sometimes they even have people driving ahead of them. The trucking company will have someone take a personal vehicle and drive ahead of the truck—almost like a blocker—so that they can radio back to the truck and say, "Look, these people are at the weigh station. Just go another route, or don't go this way, or go that way." I know it sounds like *Smokey and the Bandit*, but it's true.

In West Virginia and Ohio, we have four-lane highways like I–70, I–79, Interstate 64, Interstate 68, Interstate 77, Route 50, and Route 33—that are absolutely covered with trucks. On these roadways, the personal motor vehicle is in the minority.

From my office window, I can see thousands of trucks go by every day. While all of these trucks are supposed to stop at the weigh stations, that enforcement isn't enough. They weigh the truck and that's about it. Nobody is checking brakes there, for instance. While they do a reasonably good job of checking drivers' logs to check for fatigue, there's no assurance that those logs are accurate to begin with. I would question their authenticity. As I've described in this book, I have had cases where the driver's logs were deliberately misrepresented. The loads on these trucks aren't being secured the way they should be. Often the tires are worn and don't have sufficient tread, because it costs too much money to replace these tires.

In today's large tractor trailers, if you started on the East Coast with full tanks of fuel, you could almost drive across the entire United States stopping only once or twice for additional fuel. Think about that. You could go across the country and stop for fuel once, maybe twice. It's incredible. These tanks can hold 150 gallons each, 125 to 150 gallons a side. The regulations are hard to enforce, because in the end the trucking company has to self-enforce, and they are not going to do that. They're not doing it now, and they're not going to do it in the future.

There is a danger that additional legislation could make it worse. Reform legislation that limits the amounts of liability—the cost to the trucking company if they hurt or kill someone—would hurt, because then they will do even less. You can't get a trucking company to fix the brakes unless they want to, because the brakes are not being checked. No weigh station is checking the thickness of the brakes. They're not checking the load to make sure it's secure. All they do is weigh that truck, and that's assuming the company doesn't find a way to avoid even that.

This is a significant problem, and it is widespread. Even the largest trucking companies in the country, those that have the resources to police their fleet of trucks properly, are still driven by the same profit-over-safety mentality that the small companies have. It is a competitive business. The more loads you take, the more money you make, and the happier your customer is. And a happy customer will call you to move new loads.

So the trucking companies have a financial incentive against complying with rules and regulations regarding their trucks. The same incentive applies when it comes to drivers. There is a lack of qualified drivers. The opioid epidemic that has swept the whole country in recent years has hit West Virginia and Ohio especially hard, and it has affected the labor pool for every business, including trucking companies. Qualified truck drivers who are both drug-free and accident-free are difficult to find, so those drivers who *are* qualified are being pushed to their limit, not because they want to be pushed so hard, but because the companies leave them no choice. The trucking company doesn't want to look too closely. They don't want to know for sure how many hours that truck driver has driven, because if they find out that he's driven too many hours, they will have to pull him off the road for eight hours, and they don't want to do that. They're better off not knowing. If they let the burden remain on the driver, then they can blame the driver when something happens.

It's always to the benefit of the trucking company to turn a blind eye. Then they can say, "Gee, we didn't know. We didn't know that the driver had driven 16 hours. We didn't know that the tires were worn out. We didn't know the brakes were worn out. If we had known, we would have done something about it." Then they can blame the truck driver himself or herself. The companies will do or say anything to avoid taking responsibility for their own wrongful conduct. They will blame the victim, they will blame their own driver, they will blame the weather, and they will blame the mechanic. They will blame everyone and everything, but they will not take responsibility.

Financial incentives also motivate the drivers of these trucks. They don't make very much money—I was shocked to learn how little they make—and they get paid by the mile.

It's a tough job. These guys are living on the road all the time, they don't get to see their families, they're in a safety-sensitive job, and they make very little money. I had a case where the driver was getting paid 38 cents per mile. Then he moved up to a new job making 42 cents per mile.

Let's do a little bit of math. Suppose you drove 100,000 miles a year. At 42 cents a mile, you'd be making $42,000. That doesn't seem like a lot of money for 100,000 miles a year. Most people don't drive that many miles in five years. This company that is paying its drivers 42 cents a mile is a national trucking company. Well, if you're only getting paid 42 cents a mile, you have all the incentive in the world to drive as many miles as you possibly can, even if it means bending the rules.

You might think that trucking companies might offer their drivers an incentive for maintaining a clean, accident-free driving record. I know of a company that had an incentive program like that. This was the incentive: If you had 100,000 miles of accident-free driving time, your bonus was that you got to have lunch with the boss. What kind of incentive is that? Apparently that boss thought pretty highly of himself. His drivers were less impressed.

It should be clear that all of the economic incentives, for both the trucking companies and their drivers, work toward making this epidemic of trucking collisions worse, not better. That's why the driving public needs to be informed about the dangers and what to do if they should find themselves caught up in one of these incidents.

What's the bottom line?

There are no happy endings in these cases. These are often catastrophic events and something that we never want to happen to anyone. But when it does happen, my goal is always to make the end result as favorable to the client and the clients family as it can be. I can't take away someone's pain, but I can help them put their life back together.

No one is happy that they were involved in a collision with a truck. No family member has ever lost a loved one in a trucking collision and then, at the end of the case, been happy.

What we do for clients is help put their lives back together financially. The results of the case are what matter here. These settlements and these verdicts help to pay the medical expenses. They replace the lost wages. They provide lifetime care for people who have been severely and permanently injured. That's what makes our job so rewarding.

In the Introduction to this book I told you about the Donna Collins case. That case was settled a few months ago for $18,250,000.

At the end of the day, we were able to do what we promised we would do. We promised the family of this young woman who was horribly injured, and who now needs lifetime care for traumatic brain injury, that we would make sure this company took responsibility and paid what they needed to pay to take care of her. If you were to ask the Collins family, they would tell you that we did what we promised we would do.

Of course they are never going to be happy with the fact that their daughter was severely injured in a trucking accident. But they are satisfied that now they have the financial resources to take care of this poor woman for the rest of her life. Donna was only 46 years old at the time of the collision. She had no children and was not married. There was no one to care for her. Her parents were in their early 70s. The parents aren't going to be around forever. Who's going to take care of her when they are gone? We were able to remove the financial burden and worry for that family.

We're able to lift the financial burden of these horrific tragedies off of their shoulders. That's why people come to us. We can't fix their broken hearts. We can't fix their injuries. What we *can* do is put them in a better place financially. We can put them in a place where they are more comfortable, where they can live a reasonably normal life, and where there are resources to take care of their needs. That's what we do, and at the risk of sounding arrogant, I actually think we're pretty good at it.

There is seldom a trucking collision that doesn't result in a serious injury or death. Nobody gets a whiplash injury from a trucking accident. It's always a very serious incident, and so you need people who are experienced in this type of law, with these types of damages and these types of issues, to get the result that you're really going to need for the rest of your life. It's that important.

These incidents are life-changing, and the selection of a lawyer in a trucking case can also be life-changing. That sounds dramatic, but it's the truth. Our job is to help people reassemble their life. We help them try to get them back to where they were, or as close to that as possible.

Here's one last example: We're dealing with a client right now who was paralyzed as the result of his truck accident. He is confined to a wheelchair. This guy likes to hunt deer. He's always been a deer hunter, and one of the things he misses the most is being able to go and hunt deer. He's got a powered wheelchair, but of course the wheelchair has wheels. He can't use it for hunting; the wheels would sink into the mud and grass as he tried to get out to the field.

We're working on getting him a tracked wheelchair, one that he can take out into the woods so he can hunt. He's not going to be able to climb into a tree stand the way he used to do, but he's going to be able to hunt out of that tracked wheelchair. We're having it set up now so there will be a rest for his gun, because we want to try to put him back in the position he was in before this accident.

I can't make it possible for him to walk again. I wish I could; I would do anything if I could help him to walk again, but I can't. What I can do is help him, so that he lives as close to a normal life as he can. We got him a wheelchair-accessible van. We're getting him the tracked wheelchair. We're making modifications to his house, so that he can live as normal a life as possible. That's our job.

That's what Colombo Law is all about. I often say that we handle the big and the bad. People throughout West Virginia and Ohio call on us when they're involved in something big and bad. Collisions between personal vehicles and tractor-trailers or other commercial vehicle collisions are typically big and bad, and the smaller personal vehicle always gets the worst of it.

We're the law firm that people throughout West Virginia and Ohio call upon to handle the big and the bad and the complicated and the emotional and the expensive and the difficult. We are involved when the stakes are high. We work on all kinds of cases, but we have a primary focus on trucking cases. Those are the kinds of cases that we handle.

I speak around the country on these issues, and as I was preparing for a recent talk, I took a look back over our recent history. In the last five years, we've settled over $60 million in cases.

What I'm most proud of, though, is that our clients are happy with us, and that our clients will tell you that we do what we say we will do. That's far more important to me than the money. That's far more important to me than $60 million in five years.

Our clients will tell you that we do what we promised them we would do. They're happy with our representation, and they ultimately become ambassadors for our law firm. While we do advertise on TV and on the internet, our best cases come as referrals from past clients and people who know us.

There's no bigger honor than that: to receive a referral from a past client, someone who has been through one of these horrible collisions but has been helped by our firm. When someone calls me and says, "I'm hurt bad . . ." or "My wife . . . my daughter . . . my husband has been killed. I need you," and "you were recommended by so and so," there's no bigger honor than that for me.

I have been doing this work for almost 30 years. This is a

business, of course, and it is my livelihood. It has provided me with a good living, for which I am very grateful. But at the end of the day, those referrals and testimonials—knowing that I have helped people reassemble their lives after catastrophes—are far more important to me than the financial reward.

In this book, I have tried to share the important lessons I have learned over the years of dealing with these devastating collisions. I hope that you never have to put these lessons to use, but if you do, know that you do not have to deal with it alone. We are here, and we will help.

About the Author

Dino S. Colombo has been litigating complex personal injury and wrongful death cases for past 28 years. He is routinely involved in cases where permanent injuries, including brain injury and significant physical deformity, are involved. Mr. Colombo has tried many cases to verdict and has handled numerous appeals. He and his team are consulted by lawyers from around the country when assistance is needed in working up and trying complex cases where the damages are in the millions of dollars.

Mr. Colombo is on the Executive Committee of the National Trial Lawyers, is in the Top 100 Trial Lawyers as designated by the National Trial Lawyers, is a West Virginia Super Lawyer, is a member of the Academy of Truck Accident Attorneys, is a Board Member of the Association of Plaintiff Interstate Trucking Lawyers of America, is a member of the American Association of Justice and the TAOS Group. Mr. Colombo resides in Morgantown, WV with his wife and two children. He is an outdoorsman and enjoys traveling.

http://www.callcolombolaw.com/attorneys/dino-colombo/

Testimonials

"It amazed me that Dino would take on a company that size, but he did. He took care of it. He got the insurance company to reimburse me for all of my damages and time lost. I can't say enough good things about him."

— Ralph

....

"Dino had the ability to not only go out for what was owed to us, but also to get what we deserved. It made a difference that he was willing to go the extra mile to provide relief for us."

— Latricia

....

"You can't negotiate with an insurance company. You have to have something more–that is when Dino came in. Thank god for Dino. He was just marvelous. He cared so much. I don't know what we would have done without him."

— Joe & Roseanne

....

"I wouldn't have known which way to turn or what to do but there was no worried, Dino took care of it."

— Sabrina

....

"He's not like any other lawyer, he's a grade above."

— Mike

....

"After we made contact with Dino and he saw what we were going through, he took charge and there was never any question about it."

— Steve

....

"The first meeting I had with him, he told me that there would be no money due until the case is settled. That takes a huge burden off your back. He's the guy that you always want on your side, you don't ever want to be on the other side of him."

— John

....

"From the very beginning this has never been about the money, this has been about the product and what it did to my child. And Dino was determined to see that that product never hurt anyone else."

— Kim

....

"We had contacted Dino because we knew that there was wrongdoing in the company. Something needed to be done not just for our family, but to help prevent it."

— Rebecca

....